CRIMINAL JUSTICE

IN PENNSYLVANIA

ELLEN G. COHN

Florida International University

PEARSON

Prentice
Hall

Upper Saddle River, New Jersey 07458

Executive Editor: Frank Mortimer, Jr.
Assistant Editor: Sarah Holle
Production Editor: Barbara Cappuccio
Director of Manufacturing and Production: Bruce Johnson
Managing Editor: Mary Carnis
Manufacturing Buyer: Cathleen Petersen
Creative Director: Cheryl Asherman
Cover Design Coordinator: Miguel Ortiz
Cover Design: Denise Brown
Cover Image: Day Williams/Photo Researchers, Inc.

Pearson Prentice Hall™ is a trademark of Pearson Education, Inc.
Pearson® is a registered trademark of Pearson plc
Prentice Hall® is a registered trademark of Pearson Education, Inc.

Pearson Education LTD.
Pearson Education Singapore, Pte. Ltd
Pearson Education, Canada, Ltd
Pearson Education–Japan
Pearson Education Australia PTY, Limited
Pearson Education North Asia Ltd
Pearson Educaçion de Mexico, S.A. de C.V.
Pearson Education Malaysia, Pte. Ltd

10 9 8 7

ISBN 0-13-170166-5

CONTENTS

PREFACE

This text will provide you with specific information on the Pennsylvania criminal justice system and the Pennsylvania criminal law. Throughout the book, you will find a number of quotations which have been taken verbatim from various legal documents, such as the Pennsylvania Consolidated Statutes and the Pennsylvania Constitution. Any misspellings or other irregularities are reproduced exactly as they appear in the original documents.

I hope that you enjoy this book and find it both interesting and informative. If you have any questions, comments, or suggestions, please feel free to contact me.

Ellen G. Cohn, Ph.D.
cohne@fiu.edu

CHAPTER 1

THE COMMONWEALTH OF PENNSYLVANIA

INTRODUCTION

The Commonwealth of Pennsylvania is located in the Middle Atlantic region of the United States. It is bounded by New York and Lake Erie on the north, New York and New Jersey on the east, Delaware, Maryland, and West Virginia on the south, and West Virginia and Ohio on the west. The capital of Pennsylvania is Harrisburg and the largest city in the state is Philadelphia. The state bird is the ruffed grouse; the state flower is the mountain laurel; the state tree is the hemlock; and the official state beverage is milk. Pennsylvania's nickname is the "Keystone State."[1]

THE HISTORY OF PENNSYLVANIA

The Pre-Colonial Period

Pennsylvania was originally occupied by a number of Native American groups, including the Delaware and the Susquehannock. During the late 17th century the Shawnee also moved into Pennsylvania.

The first recorded visits to Pennsylvania by European explorers was in the early 17th century. In 1608, Captain John Smith visited the Susquehannock Indians and in 1609 Henry Hudson sailed into Delaware Bay. In approximately 1615 or 1616, French explorer Etienne Brule explored the Susquehanna River while Dutch explorer Cornelius Hendricksen sailed up the Delaware River. A trading post was established on the Schuylkill River in 1633 by Dutch settlers based on Manhattan Island. The first permanent settlement was established in 1643, by a Swedish expedition who set up New Sweden. Conflict arose between the Dutch, who by this time had set up several trading posts, and the Swedish settlers and in 1655, the Dutch took over the region and made it part of their New Netherland colony. New Netherland was captured by the British in 1664 and the entire region (which would eventually include the colonies of New York, New Jersey, Pennsylvania, and Delaware) was renamed New York.

Pennsylvania as an English Colony

In the late 1600s William Penn petitioned King Charles II of England for a land grant. His goal was to set up a colony for Quakers suffering religious persecution. King Charles signed the Charter of Pennsylvania in 1681, granting Penn a portion of the New York colony. The colony was named by the King in honor of William Penn's father, Admiral Sir William Penn. The following year, Penn also received an area known as the Lower Counties, which is now the state of Delaware. Settlers in Pennsylvania were promised religious tolerance and the ability to participate in colonial government and Quakers from England, Wales, and Holland quickly arrived in the region. They were followed by a large number of German Amish and Mennonite settlers in the early 1700s, who were fleeing from religious persecution in their own country. The region in which they settled is now known as Pennsylvania Dutch country, from the word "Deutsch," which means "German." Scotch-Irish immigrants also settled in the new colony in response to economic difficulties in Ireland. By 1776, Pennsylvania had approximately 300,000 inhabitants.

In 1681, William Markham was named deputy governor of Pennsylvania by William Penn. Penn also drafted a document known as the First Frame of Government, which was a contract between himself and the colonists. In 1682, Penn visited the city of Philadelphia, which was still under construction, and called together the colony's first General Assembly, which approved the Frame of Government. A second Assembly, which met in 1683, revised the First Frame and created the Second Frame of Government, increasing the power of the settlers in colonial government. The Frame of Government gave settlers freedom of worship, protection of property, trial by jury, and guaranteed all Christian men over 21 years of age who owned property or paid a personal tax a right to participate in colonial government. In 1692, after the English Revolution, King William III and Queen Mary, rulers of England, revoked Penn's charter over the colony of Pennsylvania. It was restored in 1694 and the Penn family remained proprietors of the colony until American independence. Penn's heirs abandoned the Quaker religion, creating frequent conflict between the Penn family and the General Assembly, which included many Quakers.

During the late 1600s and early 1700s, Pennsylvania participated in the various wars between France and England. The French and Indian War began on July 1754 in Pennsylvania when George Washington's forces were defeated by the French in the Battle of Fort Necessity. The following year British troops were defeated by French and Native American troops at Fort Duquesne near the Ohio River. Members of the Shawnee and Delaware tribes, angered by a 1754 treaty between the Pennsylvania colonists and the Iroquois that gave the colonists land occupied by the tribes, rampaged over the Pennsylvania frontier, killing settlers and burning houses and crops. In response, the General Assembly approved funds to construct a series of forts to defend the colony. More battles were fought in Pennsylvania during the following three years, ending when Fort Duquesne was retaken from the French by General John Forbes. The fort was renamed Pittsburgh. That same year, the colony entered into a peace treaty with the Iroquois, returning the land that had been purchased by the colony in 1754, and ending the attacks on the colony by the Delaware and Shawnee.

In 1763, Pontiac, chief of the Ottawa people, captured 10 of the 14 British forts located between Lake Superior and the Pennsylvania frontier. Pontiac's War ended in August after the Native Americans were defeated at Bushy Run. However, in December, a group of men from the village of Paxton (located in eastern Pennsylvania, near Harrisburg) attacked a settlement of Susquehannocks near Lancaster. Although they had not participated in Pontiac's War, the Paxton Boys killed a total of 20 members of the tribe, including women, children, and elderly men.

The American Revolution

In the 1760s, Parliament attempted to raise money to pay off war debts by levying a number of taxes on the American colonies. The 1764 Sugar Act, the 1765 Stamp Act, and others led to anger and protests on the part of the colonists. However, Pennsylvania was somewhat less defiant than many other colonies, due in part to the ongoing conflicts between the British proprietary government and the General Assembly (which was led by Benjamin Franklin). The passage of the Townsend Acts in 1765 led to the publication of a series of protest essays by John Dickinson, a lawyer in Philadelphia. Although the Townsend Acts were repealed in 1770, the tax on tea remained and the 1773 Tea Act created further resentment among the American colonists. Although Philadelphians did not actually dump British tea into the sea, they did boycott English tea and, in one instance, the captain of the British ship *Polly* was threatened with tarring and feathering and forced to return to Britain with his cargo of tea still on board.

In 1774, the First Continental Congress assembled in Philadelphia to protest British treatment of Massachusetts after the Boston Tea Party. The Continental Congress organized a boycott of English goods and sent a declaration, drafted by John Dickinson, to the king outlining the colonies' grievances at the way they were being treated by England. The Second Continental Congress assembled the following year with Benjamin Franklin serving as a delegate from Pennsylvania. Franklin also helped to draft the Declaration of Independence, which was adopted in the State House, now known as Independence Hall.

In 1776, Pennsylvania also ratified a new constitution, which was considered the most democratic in the colonies. The constitution allowed all free white men who paid taxes to vote, eliminating the property ownership requirement. It created a unicameral legislature, with representation based on the population of each county, and an executive council instead of a state governor.

The first military action in Pennsylvania took place in December 1776, when Washington's army camped on the western bank of the Delaware River, in Morrisville, during a retreat from New Jersey. On December 25, the army re-crossed the river, launched a surprise attack on the British, and successfully defeated them in Trenton, New Jersey. In the summer of 1777, the British invaded Pennsylvania and advanced to Philadelphia. The Continental Congress fled to Lancaster and later moved to York. On September 11, 1777, the British defeated the Americans in the Battle of Brandywine. On September 25, British troops under the command of General William Howe occupied Philadelphia. On October 4, Washington launched a surprise attack against the British, in an attempt to force them out of Philadelphia. Although the Americans were defeated at the Battle of Germantown, this battle helped to persuade the French to form an alliance with the Americans. Washington's army spent the winter of 1777-1778 encamped at Valley Forge, Pennsylvania. In the spring of 1778, the British left Philadelphia and the Continental Congress returned to the city. No further major Revolutionary War battles took place in Pennsylvania, although there were a number of British and Indian raids carried out along the Pennsylvania frontier.

Postwar Pennsylvania

In the early 1700s, approximately 4,000 slaves had been brought to Pennsylvania by colonists. By 1790, there were approximately 10,000 African Americans in the state; of these, approximately 6,300 had been freed. In 1780, the state passed the Pennsylvania Gradual Abolition Act, the first emancipation statute in the country.

In 1781, the Articles of Confederation were adopted in the United States. However, the document had many flaws and in 1787 a Federal Constitutional Convention met in Philadelphia and drafted the Constitution of the United States. Pennsylvania sent a total of eight delegates to the Convention, including Benjamin Franklin and James Wilson. Although some of the revolutionary leaders in Pennsylvania opposed the new Constitution, because of their fear of centralized government, on December 12, 1787, Pennsylvania became the second state to ratify the Constitution.

Following the ratification of the United States Constitution, a state constitutional convention convened to rewrite the Constitution of Pennsylvania. The new document was modeled after the federal constitution and provided for a bicameral legislature and an elected governor (replacing the unicameral legislature and executive counsel established by the Constitution of 1776).

Between 1790 and 1800, Philadelphia served as the capital of the United States, until it was moved to Washington, D.C. It was also the capital of Pennsylvania. In 1799, the state capital was moved from Philadelphia to Lancaster; in 1812, it was moved again to Harrisburg.

Pennsylvania voters supported the Federalist Party during Washington's presidency. However, in 1791 a federal law was passed imposing an excise tax on whiskey. Grain farmers in western Pennsylvania resisted the tax, which they found a significant economic burden. In 1794, President Washington responded to the Whiskey Rebellion by calling out the militia to suppress the rebels. Washington's actions in the Whiskey Rebellion contributed to the development of an anti-Federalist movement in Pennsylvania and during the 1796 presidential election, Thomas Jefferson, a Democratic-Republican, received more votes in Pennsylvania than Federalist John Adams. In 1800, Jefferson won the presidential election and the Federalist Party fell out of power.

Pennsylvania in the 19th Century

Pennsylvania played an important role in the War of 1812, which lasted from 1812 to 1815. Pennsylvania congressman Albert Gallatin, who served as Secretary of the Treasury from 1801 to 1814, helped organize the country's finances for the war effort. He then served as a peace commissioner during the peace negotiations between the United States and Great Britain, and was significantly involved in drawing up the Treaty of Ghent, which ended the war. Other Pennsylvanians who played important roles in the War of 1812 included military leaders General Jacob Brown and Commodore Stephen Decatur.

After the war, Pennsylvania Jeffersonians split into two factions during the presidential election of 1824. Votes were split between John Quincy Adams and Andrew Jackson. Jackson received the most electoral votes but did not achieve a majority. As required by the 12th Amendment to the United States Constitution, the election was decided by the House of Representatives, which elected Adams as president. Adams ran for re-election in 1828 against Jefferson, who achieved a decisive victory due in part to the support of Pennsylvanian Democrats. However, Jackson's political policies, particularly his opposition towards rechartering the Second Bank of the United States, which was based in Philadelphia, alienated many Pennsylvanians. In 1835, a combination of the Whig Party and the anti-Masonic Party took control of state politics away from Jacksonian Democrats.

In 1837, a state constitutional convention was called and a new constitution was adopted the following year. The constitution of 1838 removed some of the appointive powers of the state governor, shortened terms of office for elected officials, and made a number of changes designed to increase the power of the voters in government. However, free African Americans were disenfranchised by the constitution.

Despite the disenfranchism clause in the new constitution, Pennsylvania was strongly opposed to slavery, which had been outlawed in the state since 1780. In 1826, the legislature passed an act designed to protect fugitive slaves and prevent them from being returned to their masters. However, in 1842 the United States Supreme Court declared the act to be unconstitutional. In 1847, another law was passed forbidding the use of jails in Pennsylvania to detain fugitive slaves. The Underground Railroad was very active in Pennsylvania, particularly along the Mason-Dixon line (the Pennsylvania-Maryland border).

In 1838, a number of reform groups, including abolitionists, built Pennsylvania Hall in Philadelphia to serve as a center for reform activities. However, the hall was burned down by anti-abolitionists soon after construction was completed. The topic of slavery became a national issue during the 1840s, eventually resulting in the passage of the Compromise of 1850 by Congress. The program included a Fugitive Slave Law that required runaway slaves be returned to their masters. In 1851, an attempt by a Maryland slave owner to use the law to regain custody of several slaves living in Lancaster County led to the Christiana Riot. During the riot, the slave owner was killed.

The passage of the Kansas-Nebraska Act in 1854 resulted in the repeal of the Missouri Compromise, which banned slavery in new territories north of the Mason-Dixon line. Pennsylvania abolitionists were so angered by this that they organized a new Republican Party in the state. The party was not strong enough to gain control during the election of 1856, when Democrat James Buchanan was elected president. Buchanan is the only native Pennsylvanian to hold the position of President of the United States. However, in 1860, the Republicans dominated both state and national elections; Republican Andrew Gregg Curtin was elected governor of Pennsylvania and Abraham Lincoln was elected president. Interestingly, the Republican party feared that the Democratic hold on the state was so great that a Republican candidate could not win in Pennsylvania so Lincoln was presented as the People's Party candidate.

The Civil War began in April 1861 and most people in Pennsylvania supported the Union, regardless of their political affiliations. Governor Curtin played a significant role in the war by organizing and hosting the Altoona Conference of 1862 in which governors of fourteen northern states pledged their personal and official support to President Lincoln and agreed to support a national draft. United States Senator Simon Cameron of Pennsylvania served as Lincoln's first Secretary of War. Pennsylvanians were active in the fighting as well. Lincoln originally called for 14 regiments of volunteers from Pennsylvania; 25 regiments responded. Over 350,000 Pennsylvania troops served in the Union forces, including over 8,600 African American volunteers. The state's industry also contributed to the war effort, building ships and producing weapons for the Union forces.

The famous Battle of Gettysburg, which is considered to be a major turning point in the Civil War, took place in Pennsylvania. General Robert E. Lee advanced on Pennsylvania in June 1863. In response, fortifications were built at Pittsburgh and Harrisburg. Eventually, on July 1, 1863 Southern troops met Union forces, commanded by General George G. Meade, at Gettysburg. Almost a third of Meade's forces were Pennsylvania troops. The battle lasted three days and resulted in almost 50,000 casualties. On November 19, during the dedication of the Gettysburg National Cemetery, Lincoln's Gettsyburg Address was delivered.

Another major battle fought in Pennsylvania was the Battle of Chambersburg, which occurred in July 1864. In response to the destruction of the Virginia Military Institute in June by Union troops, Confederate forces entered the town of Chambersburg and demanded a ransom of $500,000 in U.S. currency or $100,00 in gold. The demand was made at dawn and Confederate General John McCausland stated that if the money was not paid, the town would be burned. When the money was not produced by 9:00 A.M., Southern troops torched the town, destroying over 500 buildings, leaving two-thirds of the town's residents homeless, and causing approximately two million dollars in damage.

The Republican Party continued to dominate Pennsylvanian politics after the Civil War. Between 1861 and 1935, only one Democrat held the office of governor of Pennsylvania (Robert E. Pattison, who served from 1883 to 1887 and from 1891 to 1895). In 1874, a new constitution was adopted, which included provisions for the election of the State Treasurer, the Auditor General, and judges. The office of Lieutenant Governor was created by this constitution as well and the term of office for the governor was extended to four years. The constitution also allowed for the creation of a variety of new government agencies, leading to the creation of the Superior Court in 1895, in response to the increasingly large caseload of the state Supreme Court.

In 1859, oil was discovered at Titusville, which encouraged the development of large national corporations, including John D. Rockefeller's Standard Oil Company. The iron and steel industry was dominated by Andrew Carnegie, who built the world's largest steel mill just outside Pittsburgh. Workers in the steel and oil refineries worked seven days a week, 12 hours a day. As a result, Pennsylvania was important in the development of the national labor movement as workers attempted to unionize to obtain better working conditions, a shorter work week, and higher wages. One of the first major unions in the United States, the Knights of Labor, was founded by a Philadelphia garment worker, Uriah Stephens, in 1869. Stephens served as leader of the union until 1883 and was succeeded by Terence V. Powderly, later mayor of Scranton.

The Great Railroad Strike of 1877, which was the first national labor strike in the United States, was sparked by the poor treatment of Pennsylvania rail workers. After the Pennsylvania Railroad cut wages and increased the number of trains to be run by the same number of workers, Pittsburgh rail workers went on strike. The local militia sided with the striking workers and a militia was brought in from Philadelphia to break the strike. The Philadelphia militia fired on the strikers and on the watching crowds, killing over twenty people, including women and children. The crowds attacked the militia and set fire to the rail yards, destroying buildings, engines, and railroad cars, and causing over four million dollars in damage. The strike expanded throughout the country, shutting down approximately two-thirds of the country's rail track. Riots took place in various Pennsylvania cities, including Pittsburgh, Scranton, Reading, and Wilkes-Barre. The strike lasted until August, when it was broken by the combined force of state militia units and the United States Army. This was the first time in the history of the United States that federal troops were deployed against civilians participating in a labor strike.

After the Civil War, a group of Irish immigrants working in the coal mines in Scranton organized a secret society known as the Molly Maguires. The group focused on improving the working and living conditions of the miners and frequently used force and violence against the mine owners and the police, who were controlled by the mine owners. The group organized a union in 1875 and called a strike. Their power was broken in 1877, when Franklin B. Gowan, the president of the Reading Railroad, hired the Pinkerton Detective Agency to infiltrate and spy on the union, and eventually smashed the organization. Many of the Molly Maguire's leaders were convicted of various criminal activities and were hanged.

On May 31, 1889, one of the worst floods in the history of the United States inundated the steel mining town of Johnstown, Pennsylvania. The breaking of the South Fork Dam resulted in over 2,200 deaths and approximately seventeen million dollars in property damage.

Pennsylvania in the 20th Century

Between 1900 and 1910, an influx of European immigrants significantly increased the population of Pennsylvania. Prior to the Civil War, the majority of the state's population included northern European immigrants (Germans, English, Irish, and Scotch-Irish). However, after the turn of the century, immigrants from Finland, Italy, and Scandinavia, as well as a large number of Jewish immigrants, arrived in the state. African American migration from the South also increased, particularly after 1917. During World War I, over 300,000 Pennsylvanians served in the armed forces and Pennsylvania shipyards, factories, and mills produced needed war materials.

In the 1930s, the Great Depression significantly impacted Pennsylvanian industries and approximately one-third of all families in the state required some form of relief by 1932. The economic decline allowed the state Democratic Party, which supported President Franklin D. Roosevelt's economic relief programs, to take control of state government. In 1935, Democrat George H. Earle was elected governor and based his administration on Roosevelt's New Deal. In 1940, the Republicans regained control of the state. However, during the late 1930's, Pennsylvania played a key role in the creation of the Steel Workers Organization Committee, which became the United Steel Workers of America in 1942.

Approximately 1.25 million Pennsylvanians served in the armed forces of the United States during World War II, a figure equal to approximately one-eighth of the state's population at that time. Essentially, approximately one out of every seven members of the armed forces was a Pennsylvanian. Over 33,000 Pennsylvanians were killed in World War II. A total of 130 general and admirals were from Pennsylvania and many of the most important posts in the armed forces were held by Pennsylvanians, including the offices of the Army Chief of Staff, the Commander of the Army Air Forces, and the Commander of the American Strategic Air Forces in Europe. The state housed forty military and naval installations and two of the largest battleships in the world were constructed at the Philadelphia Navy Yard.

After World War II, the state fell into a period of economic decline as the reduced demand for coal forced mines to close and created increased unemployment. A number of textile mills moved to Southern states, or became automated, causing the loss of more jobs.

During the second half of the 20th century, Pennsylvania has been a two-party state. The governor's office was primarily controlled by the Republicans between 1934 and 1954, after which Democratic candidates won the next two elections. During the 1960s, the Republicans regained control of the governorship. In 1967, a state Constitutional Convention was called and the 1874 Constitution was significantly revised, allowing elected state officers (including the governor) to serve two consecutive terms. Democrat Milton Shapp, who served from 1970 to 1979, became the first governor to be eligible for re-election. Since then, control of the office of the governor has alternated between the Democrats and the Republicans.

PENNSYLVANIA TODAY

Pennsylvania is the 33rd largest state in the country, with a total land area of 44,817 square miles, as well as 490 square miles of inland waters and 749 square miles of Lake Erie over which the state has jurisdiction. It measures a maximum of 158 miles from north to south and 312 miles from east to west. The highest point of the state, located in Somerset County, is 3,213 feet above sea level.

Currently, Pennsylvania is the sixth most populous state in the country. The 2000 census reported a total population of 12,281,054, an increase of 3.4 percent over the 1990 figure. The state has a population density of 274.0 persons per square mile.[2] The most populous city in Pennsylvania is Philadelphia, with a population of 1,517,550 in 2000. It is the fifth largest city in the United States.

Other cities with a population of over 100,000 include Pittsburgh, Allentown, and Erie. Pennsylvania has a total of 67 counties. The largest is Philadelphia (a consolidated city-county), with a population of over 1.5 million; the smallest is Forest County, with a population of 4,946.[3]

Approximately 85.4 percent of the state's population are white and 10.0 percent are black. Approximately 3.2 percent of the population are reported as being of Hispanic origin, although they may be of any race. This is significantly lower than the national average of 12.5 percent. Approximately 15.6 percent of the population is above the age of 64; only Florida has a greater percentage of population aged 65 or above.[4]

Pennsylvania elects 2 United States Senators and 19 members of the House of Representatives, for a total of 21 electoral votes. The current state constitution was adopted in 1968.

NOTES

1. Pennsylvania Historical and Museum Commission web site (http://www.phmc.state.pa.us/)
2. U.S. Census Bureau (http://www.census.gov)
3. *The Pennsylvania Manual*, volume 116
   (http://www.dgs.state.pa.us/pamanual/site/default.asp)
4. U.S. Census Bureau, *op cit.*

CHAPTER 2

INTRODUCTION TO PENNSYLVANIA CRIMINAL LAW

THE STRUCTURE OF THE GOVERNMENT

Pennsylvania criminal law is found in the state constitution and in the Pennsylvania Code. Both have been frequently modified, amended, and altered over the past three hundred years. Pennsylvania is officially a **Commonwealth**, one of only four states in the country which are so designated (the others are Virginia, Kentucky, and Massachusetts). Today, there is no legal difference between the terms "state" and "commonwealth."[1]

The first **Constitution of Pennsylvania** was ratified in 1776, shortly after the signing of the Declaration of Independence. However, the government created by this constitution, while extremely democratic, was fairly weak, including a unicameral legislature and an executive council instead of a state governor. A new constitution was ratified in 1790, which made significant changes to the system of government in the state. A third constitution was adopted in 1838 and the current (fourth) constitution was adopted in 1874.[2] A constitutional convention was called in 1967-1968, resulting in significant revisions to the 1874 Constitution, including the establishment of a unified judicial system. In 1972, the amended constitution was named the Constitution of 1968.

The Constitution of Pennsylvania is the primary law of the state, although, of course, it is subordinate to the United States Constitution. No criminal law or constitutional amendment enacted in Pennsylvania may conflict with or violate any individual rights which are guaranteed by the U.S. Constitution, the Bill of Rights, any other Constitutional Amendments, or any federal laws. If any part of the Constitution of Pennsylvania or legal code is found to be in conflict with the U.S. Constitution or federal statutes, the Pennsylvania enactment is unconstitutional and must be changed.

There are several different ways in which the Constitution of Pennsylvania may be amended or revised. According to Article XI of the Constitution, a new amendment may be proposed in either the Senate or the House of Representatives and must be agreed upon by a majority of the members of each house. The proposed amendment must then be published in at least two newspapers in each county three months before the next general election. After the election, it must again be approved by a majority vote of the General Assembly, must again be published statewide, and must then pass by a majority vote of the electorate.

If there is an emergency that affects the safety and welfare of Pennsylvania, an emergency amendment may be proposed in either house and must be passed by two-thirds of the members of both houses. The proposed amendment is then published in at least two newspapers in each county and, at least one month after being passed by the General Assembly, may be voted upon by the

11

electorate. This emergency procedure was used several times in the 1970s to provide emergency aid to victims of Hurricane Agnes and other major storms that affected the state.[3]

The constitution may also be revised if a **constitutional convention** is called. A constitutional convention must be submitted to the people and approved by a majority of those voting in the election. The most recent constitutional convention took place in 1967.[4]

Like most states, Pennsylvania has three branches of government: executive, legislative, and judicial. Each branch is discussed in a separate article of the Constitution of Pennsylvania.

The Executive Branch

Article IV of the Constitution discusses Pennsylvania's **executive branch**, which consists of a governor, a lieutenant governor, attorney general, auditor general, state treasurer, and superintendent of public instruction (also known as the Secretary of Education).[5] They are all elected to four-year terms and may not serve more than two consecutive terms.[6] To be elected to the officer of governor or lieutenant governor, candidates must, at the time of election, be an elector at least 30 years of age and have been resident in the state for the preceding seven years. Candidates for attorney general also must have been a member of the Bar of the Supreme Court of Pennsylvania.[7] In addition, no one who is a member of the United States Congress or who holds any federal or state office may serve simultaneously as governor, lieutenant governor, or attorney general.[8]

The executive branch also includes the governor's cabinet, which includes the directors of a number of state agencies. Members of the cabinet, who are known as Secretaries, are appointed by the governor and confirmed by the Senate. The cabinet includes the Secretary of the Commonwealth, the Adjutant General, the Secretary of Education, the Insurance Commissioner, the Secretary of Banking, the Secretary of Agriculture, the Secretary of Health, the State Police Commissioner, the Secretary of Labor and Industry, the Secretary of Public Welfare, the Secretary of Revenue, the Secretary of Commerce, the Secretary of Community Affairs, the Secretary of Transportation, the Secretary of Environmental Resources, the Secretary of General Services, the Secretary of Aging, and the Secretary of Corrections.[9]

The governor has supreme executive power in the state.[10] S/he has a variety of powers, including the power to veto legislation that has been proposed by the state legislature. However, a two-thirds vote in both houses of the legislature may override the governor's veto. The governor is the commander-in-chief of the Commonwealth's military forces, has the power to appoint the heads of various state departments and members of numerous boards and commissions, and has the power to grant pardons, commute sentences, grand reprieves, and remit fines and forfeitures in all criminal cases other than impeachments. However, s/he may not grant a pardon or commute a sentence unless there is a written recommendation from the majority of the Board of Pardons.[11]

On January 21, 2003, Edward G. Rendell, a Democrat, became the 45th governor of Pennsylvania. Governor Rendell's term expires in 2007 and he is eligible to run for a second term.

The Legislative Branch

The **state legislature**, which is known as the **General Assembly**, is discussed in Article II of the Constitution of Pennsylvania and is the lawmaking branch of the state government. The General Assembly is made up of two houses: a 40-member Senate and a 203-member House of Representatives.

Each member of the legislature represents one senatorial or representative district. Senators are elected to four-year terms and representatives are elected to terms of two years.[12] There is no limit to the number of times members of the legislature may be re-elected. To be elected to the senate, candidates must be at least 25 years old; candidates for the House of Representatives must be at least 21 years of age. All candidates for the General Assembly must be citizens of Pennsylvania, have lived in the state for at least four years, and have been a resident of the district from which they are elected for at least one year. Members of the General Assembly must live in their respective districts during their terms of office.[13] No one with a conviction for embezzlement of public money, bribery, or perjury is eligible to serve in the General Assembly.[14] The presiding officer of the Senate is known as the President pro tempore and the presiding officer of the House of Representatives is known as the Speaker.[15] A majority of either house is necessary to constitute a quorum.[16]

Meetings of the state legislature are held annually in Harrisburg. It convenes on the first Tuesday in January and then meets regularly during the year for **regular sessions**. In addition, the governor may call a **special session** of the General Assembly whenever s/he feels it is in the public interest or whenever requested by a petition of the majority of the members of each house.[17] During a special session, only legislation on those subjects that have been designated by the governor in his or her proclamation may be considered. There have been 34 special sessions of the General Assembly during the state's history.[18]

The Judicial Branch

The judicial branch of the government, which is discussed in Article V of the Constitution of Pennsylvania, contains the various Pennsylvania courts. Pennsylvania has a unified judicial system, with all courts under the supervision of the Supreme Court of the state. The court system includes the Supreme Court, two intermediate appellate courts (the Superior Court and the Commonwealth Court), the Courts of Common Pleas, and the various community courts. To serve as a justice, judge, or justice of the peace, an individual must be a member of the bar of the Supreme Court of Pennsylvania, must have lived in the jurisdiction of the court (the state of Pennsylvania for statewide courts) for at least one year prior to election or appointment, and must reside in the jurisdiction of the court while serving in office.[19]

The highest court in the state is the **Pennsylvania Supreme Court**, which is made up of seven justices. The most senior justice serves as the chief justice of the Supreme Court. Supreme Court justices are elected by the voters, serve ten-year terms, and are then eligible, by retention election, to serve another term of office. The Supreme Court has exclusive jurisdiction over appeals from final orders of the Courts of Common Pleas in a variety of cases, including all cases of felony murder and all rulings of unconstitutionality.[20] Additionally, it has the authority to issue *writs of certiorari* for those matters from the Superior or Commonwealth Courts that it desires to hear.

The **Superior Court** has exclusive jurisdiction over all other appeals from the Courts of Common Pleas and original jurisdiction over cases involving applications for wiretapping and electronic surveillance. The court has 15 judges, one of whom is elected to serve as the President Judge. Superior Court judges are elected and serve ten-year terms.[21] Most cases are heard by panels of three judges. On approval, a matter, after original decision, may be heard again by the full court (*en banc*).

The **Commonwealth Court** is also an appellate court, although it has original jurisdiction over most civil actions against the state government, civil actions by the state government or an officer of the government, and election matters relating to state offices. The court has nine judges, with one elected to serve as President Judge. They serve ten-year terms and may then run for retention and serve a second ten-year term. In addition, six senior judges of the Supreme Court are designated to sit with the Commonwealth Court.[22] Most decisions are rendered by panels of three judges although certain matters may be reviewed by the entire court.

The **Philadelphia Municipal Court** has criminal jurisdiction over crimes with a punishment that involves imprisonment for no more than five years, crimes for which no prison term may be imposed, and some more serious offenses under motor vehicle law. The court also has some civil jurisdiction. The **Traffic Court of Philadelphia** has exclusive jurisdiction over most violations of motor vehicle ordinances or violations of state motor vehicle laws committed within Philadelphia County.[23]

District Justices were formerly known as **Justices of the Peace**. They have jurisdiction over offenses that involve driving under the influence, certain misdemeanors, civil claims involving sums of no more than $8,000, and various summary offenses not within the jurisdiction of a traffic court. They may also preside at arraignments, fix bail, and issue warrants.[24]

Each judicial district has at least one **Court of Common Pleas**, which has jurisdiction over all civil and criminal actions and proceedings, unless another court has exclusive original jurisdiction. The Court of Common Pleas within each district may be divided up into administrative units known as divisions. Each district must have a trial division, but larger districts may have multiple divisions. For example, the Court of Common Pleas of Philadelphia County has three divisions: the trial division, the orphans' court division, and the family court division. The trial division is further subdivided into civil and criminal components.[25]

Passing a Law in Pennsylvania

In Pennsylvania, a bill may be introduced in either the House or the Senate and, after it has been passed by one of the two legislative houses, it may still be amended in the other. The legislator who sponsors the bill sends the proposal to the **Legislative Reference Bureau**, which is responsible for drafting and publishing laws in the proper format. The bill is then given a number and will be assigned to a **Standing Committee** for study and review. The committee essentially performs an initial screening; many bills are stopped in committee and are never considered. During the review process, the committee may hold meetings, which are open to the public, to discuss the bill. The bill may also be referred to a subcommittee for further study. The committee eventually votes and may table the bill (making it inactive, amend the bill, defeat or fail the bill, or accept the bill).

If the bill is passed, it may go through a second review process in the **Caucus Room**. This allows each political party to discuss the bill with the members of that party. Eventually, the bill will be reported to the Floor of the House or Senate. The full legislative house must consider the bill three separate times before taking a final vote. The first day of consideration involves announcing that the bill was reported from committee and reading the number and title of the bill. On the second day of consideration, the title and number of the bill are again read to the full house. The members of the house do not debate the bill, but they do decide whether there is enough information available to discuss the bill. The third day of consideration involves a full debate on the bill. Amendments may be discussed and added, and the bill is voted on. Passage of most bills requires a majority vote from the members of the house.

If the bill passes in one house, it moves on to the other and goes through the same review process. If it is amended, it will return to the first house for a new vote. It is possible for a bill to move back and forth between the two legislative houses many times before agreement as to the final wording is obtained. If the bill passes in both houses of the General Assembly, the Speaker of the House and the President Pro Tempore of the Senate sign the bill in the presence of their respective houses.

The bill then goes to the governor for approval. The governor may sign the bill into law, fail to sign the bill (in which case it becomes a law by default), or veto the bill. The General Assembly may, by a two-thirds vote of each house, enact a bill into law over the governor's veto.[26]

PENNSYLVANIA CRIMINAL LAW

There are several sources of criminal law in Pennsylvania. These include:

- federal and state constitutions
- statutory criminal law
- case law

Together, the Constitution of Pennsylvania and the U.S. Constitution provide the basic framework for criminal law, first by focusing on individual rights and on the limitations placed on government power and second, by requiring the establishment of a judicial system. However, neither the federal nor the state constitution significantly emphasizes the creation or definition of crimes.

The primary source of **statutory criminal law** in Pennsylvania is the Pennsylvania Crimes Code, which is codified in Title 18 of the Pennsylvania Consolidated Statutes (Pa.C.S.). The state legislature has been working to create a consolidated statutory code since the late 1960s. The project is still a work in progress, with the result that only a portion of the state statutes have been published in the Pennsylvania Consolidated Statutes. The rest are still unconsolidated, making legal research somewhat confusing at the present time. Statutes that have not been consolidated are published under subject titles in Purdon's Statutes (P.S.).

The Pennsylvania Crimes Code was originally based on the English **common law**, which became the law of the original thirteen colonies and then evolved into the law of the individual states as they entered the union. However, according to the Crimes Code, "No conduct constitutes a crime unless it is a crime under this title or another statute of the Commonwealth."[27] Because of this, there are no common law crimes in Pennsylvania. For a law to be enforced, it must be written down, or codified.

The purposes of the Pennsylvania Crimes Code are outlined in 18 Pa.C.S. §104, which states that:

> The general purposes of this title are:
> (i) To forbid and prevent conduct that unjustifiably inflicts or threatens substantial harm to individual or public interest.
> (ii) To safeguard conduct that is without fault from condemnation as criminal.
> (iii)   To safeguard offenders against excessive, disproportionate or arbitrary punishment.
> (iv)   To give fair warning of the nature of the conduct declared to constitute an offense, and of the sentences that may be imposed on conviction of an offense.
> (v) To differentiate on reasonable grounds between serious and minor offenses, and to differentiate among offenders with a view to a just individualization in their treatment.

Case law consists of appellate court decisions or opinions which interpret the meaning of the law. Effectively, case law is made by judges when they hand down decisions in court. Because of the principle of *stare decisis*, or precedent, a decision made by a judge in one court will be followed by later judges in the state until the same court reverses its decision or until the decision is overturned by a higher court. However, a decision by one Court of Common Pleas is not binding upon another county court; the situation created by contradictory decisions by two Courts of Common Pleas would have to be resolved by an appellate court.

The Pennsylvania Crimes Code contains two types of statutory criminal law: substantive and procedural. **Substantive criminal laws** are those laws that define specific crimes and set forth the required punishments associated with each criminal act. The section of the Pennsylvania Statutes that defines murder is an example of substantive criminal law.[28] **Procedural laws**, on the other hand, focus on the methods that are used to enforce the substantive criminal law. In other words, procedural laws outline the rules that the state must follow when dealing with crimes and criminals. These include the procedures that must be used to investigate crimes, arrest suspects, and carry out formal prosecution. The protection against double jeopardy, which is discussed in 18 PaC.S. §109, is an example of procedural law.

THE DEFINITION AND CLASSIFICATION OF CRIME

In Pennsylvania, a **crime** is defined in 18 Pa.C.S. §106(a), which states that

> An offense defined by this title for which a sentence of death or of imprisonment is authorized constitutes a crime.

The Crimes Code classifies crimes into several categories.[29] The most serious class includes the crimes of first, second, and third degree murder as well as first, second, and third degree murder of an unborn child. The Code also recognizes three degrees of felonies:

- A **felony of the first degree** is any crime that has been so designated by statute or any crime for which the offender has been sentenced to a maximum term of imprisonment of more than ten years. Kidnapping and rape are first degree felonies.

- A **felony of the second degree** is any crime that has been so designated by statute or any crime for which the offender has been sentenced to a maximum term of imprisonment of not more than ten years. The theft of a firearm is a second degree felony.

- A **felony of the third degree** is any crime that has been so designated by statute or any crime for which the offender has been sentenced to a maximum term of imprisonment of not more than seven years. The theft of a motor vehicle is an example of a third degree felony.

Like felonies, misdemeanors are also classified by degree:

- A **misdemeanor of the first degree** is any crime that has been so designated by statute or any crime for which the offender has been sentenced to a maximum term of imprisonment of more than five years. Indecent assault of a victim under the age of 13 is a first degree misdemeanor.

- A **misdemeanor of the second degree** is any crime that has been so designated by statute or any crime for which the offender has been sentenced to a maximum term of imprisonment of not more than two years. The theft of property valued at between $50 and $200 is a second degree misdemeanor.

- A **misdemeanor of the third degree** is any crime that has been so designated by statute or any crime for which the offender has been sentenced to a maximum term of imprisonment of not more than one year. The theft of property valued at less than $50 is a third degree misdemeanor.

Pennsylvania also recognizes crimes known as **summary offenses.** While these are not included in the list of "classes of crimes" found in 18 Pa.C.S. §107(a), they are considered to be crimes because the punishment for summary offenses is imprisonment. A summary offense is any offense that is so designated by statute or for which the offender may be punished by a term of imprisonment for not more than 90 days.[30]

In some cases, the statute defining a crime may identify the crime as a felony without specifying the degree. In these cases, the crime is assumed to be a third degree felony.[31] If the crime is identified as a misdemeanor, but no degree is given, the crime is presumed to be a third degree misdemeanor.[32] If the law states that a certain behavior is a crime, but does not specify the class at all (even to identify the crime as a felony or misdemeanor), the crime is presumed to be a misdemeanor of the second degree unless the maximum sentence makes it a felony.[33]

In addition to a sentence of incarceration, convicted offenders may also be sentenced to pay a fine. 18 Pa.C.S. §1101 outlines the fines for each designated classification of crime. Sentencing and the various types of punishments used in Pennsylvania are discussed in more detail in Chapter 6.

DEFENSES TO A CRIMINAL CHARGE

There are a wide variety of defenses to a criminal charge. Many are specifically mentioned in the Pennsylvania Consolidated Statutes or have been discussed by the Pennsylvania courts.

Alibi

An **alibi** is defined as:

> ...a defense that places the defendant at the relevant time in a different place than the scene involved and so removed therefrom as to render it impossible for him to be the guilty party.[34]

An individual who uses the defense of an **alibi** essentially is claiming that s/he was elsewhere when the crime was committed and thus could not have committed the crime. For an alibi defense to be effective, it must cover the entire time period when the defendant's presence was necessary to commit the crime. There is no minimum distance requirement; as long as the defendant is physically separated from the location in such a way that it would be impossible for him or her to have committed the crime, the defense may be appropriate.[35]

Justifications

A defendant who uses a **justification** defense admits to the commission of the criminal act but also claims that it was necessary to commit the act in order to avoid some greater evil or harm.[36] Probably the most well-known justification defense is that of **self-defense**, in which the defendant claims that the use of force against the victim was justifiable because it was the only way the defendant could ensure his or her own safety. The use of force in the protection of one's self is discussed in 18 Pa.C.S. §505, which states that:

> (a) The use of force upon or toward another person is justifiable when the actor believes that such force is immediately necessary for the purpose of protecting himself against the use of unlawful force by such other person on the present occasion.

The Crimes Code also discusses the issue of **deadly force**, which is defined as "Force which, under the circumstances in which it is used, is readily capable of causing death or serious injury."[37] According to statute:

> The use of deadly force is not justifiable under this section unless the actor believes that such force is necessary to protect himself against death, serious bodily injury, kidnapping or sexual intercourse compelled by force or threat; nor is it justifiable if:
> (i) the actor, with the intent of causing death or serious bodily injury, provoked the use of force against himself in the same encounter; or
> (ii) the actor knows that he can avoid the necessity of using such force with complete safety by retreating or by surrendering possession of a thing to a person asserting a claim of right thereto or by complying with a demand that he abstain from any action which he has no duty to take...[38]

Essentially, a victim may only use deadly force if there is no other alternative. There are several exceptions to this. The most notable is the fact that the victim generally is not required to retreat if the assault takes place in his or her dwelling or place of work. This is sometimes known as the **castle doctrine**, from the old saying "A man's home is his castle." Essentially, a victim's right to protect his or her home (or place of work) supercedes the legal requirement to retreat rather than use deadly force.[39] However, if the victim is assaulted in another location, the requirement to retreat takes precedence.

In general, the amount of force that is used in self defense must be proportionate to the amount of force or threat that the defendant is experiencing. An individual is not justified in using deadly force against an assailant if s/he had no reason to believe that the assailant would cause death or serious bodily harm. The courts have stated that when an individual uses excessive force against an attacker, the claim of self defense may not be supported.[40]

Self-defense also applies to the **protection of others**. The Crimes Code also allows the use of force to protect a third person. Again, deadly force may only be used to protect a third person from death or serious bodily injury.[41]

Another justification defense is that of **consent**. This defense claims that the injured person voluntarily consented to the actions that caused the injury. According to 18 Pa.C.S.§311(a),

> The consent of the victim to conduct charged to constitute an offense or to the result thereof is a defense if such consent negatives an element of the offense or precludes the infliction of the harm or evil sought to be prevented by the law defining the offense.

The defense of consent is most commonly used in sex-related offenses, such as rape and sexual assault. Essentially, the defendant claims that the victim freely agreed to the sexual act, sexual contact, or intercourse. However, assent that is obtained from n individual who is unable to legally give consent (e.g., because of youth, intoxication, or disease) or that is obtained by force, duress, deception, or coercion, is not considered to be consent under the law.[42]

Excuses

A defendant using an **excuse** defense is claiming that at the time of the criminal act some circumstance or personal condition creates a situation under which s/he should not be held criminally accountable. Probably the most well-known (and controversial) defense in this category is that of **insanity**. Although the term insanity is no longer used by mental health professionals, it is a legal term referring to a defense that is based on the defendant's claim that s/he was mentally ill or mentally incapacitated at the time of the offense.

Pennsylvania uses the **M'Naughton Rule** as a test for insanity. This requires the defendant to show by a preponderance of evidence that s/he was legally insane at the time the crime was committed.[43] The term **legally insane** is defined as:

> At the time of the commission of the offense, the actor was laboring under such a defect of reason, from disease of the mind, as not to know the nature and quality of the act he was doing or, if the actor did know the quality of the act, that he did not now that what he was doing was wrong.[44]

Pennsylvania does not recognize the **irresistible impulse test** that is used in some states.[45]

If a defendant is acquitted of criminal charges using the insanity defense, s/he will be found **not guilty by reason of insanity**. However, in some cases, a defendant who was not legally insane at the time the crime was committed may still have suffered from some type of mental illness that affected his or her behavior. In these cases, the court is allowed to return a finding of **guilty but mentally ill**. **Mentally ill** is defined as:

> One who as a result of mental disease or defect lacks substantial capacity either to appreciate the wrongfulness of his conduct or to conform his conduct to the requirements of the law.[46]

This is identical to the **substantial capacity test** for insanity that was proposed in the Model Penal Code (MPC), and that was not accepted by Pennsylvania. Essentially, if a defendant meets the requirements of the M'Naughen Test, s/he will be found not guilty by reason of insanity. If s/he does not meet these requirements, but does meet the MPC definition of mentally ill, the court will return a verdict of guilty but mentally ill.

A defendant found not guilty by reason of insanity may be committed to a psychiatric facility through a civil proceeding. A defendant found guilty but mentally ill is sentenced in the same way as if s/he was simply found guilty. However, s/he will have the right to appropriate psychiatric treatment.[47]

Another defense that falls into the category of excuses is that of **involuntary intoxication**. 18 Pa.C.S. §308 states that "Neither voluntary intoxication nor voluntary drugged condition is a defense to a criminal charge..." The statutes do not specifically address the issue of involuntary intoxication as a defense. However, case law generally holds that the law relating to voluntary intoxication does not apply when intoxication was involuntary.[48]

Duress is another excuse defense. The Crimes Code states that:

> It is a defense that the actor engaged in the conduct charged to constitute an offense because he was coerced to do so by the use of, or a threat to use, unlawful force against his person or the person of another, which a person of reasonable firmness in his situation would have been unable to resist.[49]

Effectively, if the defendant commits a crime under some type of threat of imminent death or great bodily harm, s/he is not guilty of the offense. The theory behind the defense is that the duress removes the defendant's free will and therefore negates the element of intent or *mens rea* that is required for the crime. Duress is an acceptable defense for practically all criminal activity, although there is some debate in the courts as to whether may be accepted as a defense in the crime of first degree murder in Pennsylvania.

Procedural Defenses

A **procedural defense** claims that some form of official procedure was not followed or that procedural law was not properly followed during the investigation or the prosecution of the crime.

One procedural defense is that of **double jeopardy**. Article I, Section 10 of the Pennsylvania Constitution states that "No person shall, for the same offense, be twice put in jeopardy of life or limb...." The Fifth Amendment to the United States Constitution provides the same protection. Therefore, an individual may not be prosecuted a second time for an offense if s/he already has been convicted or acquitted of that offense. The issue of double jeopardy may be grounds for the defense to make a pretrial motion to dismiss the case.

Another procedural defense is **entrapment**. According to the Crimes Code,

> A public law enforcement official or a person acting in cooperation with such an official perpetrates an entrapment if for the purpose of obtaining evidence of the commission of an offense, he induces or encourages another person to engage in conduct constituting such offense by either:
> (1) making knowingly false representations designed to induce the belief that such conduct is not prohibited; or
> (2) employing methods of persuasion or inducement which create a substantial risk that such an offense will be committed by persons other than those who are ready to commit it.[50]

Basically, an individual using the entrapment defense is claiming the behavior of law enforcement officers induced him or her to commit the illegal act. The focus shifts to the conduct of the police and the defense is designed to act as a deterrent for police misconduct, based on the belief that it is better to allow some offenders to escape punishment than to allow police officers to behave illegally. The defendant must prove entrapment by a preponderance of the evidence.[51]

The entrapment defense is most commonly used when the defendant was ensnared in an undercover police action, usually relating to the sale of illegal drugs. In general, the defendant will claim that s/he does not regularly sell drugs but made a sale as a favor to the undercover officer. One of the most common ways for the police to prevent the use of this defense is to make two or more purchases from the same suspect; after the suspect has made multiple sales, the jury is more likely to believe that the undercover officer simply provided the defendant with an opportunity to commit the crime, rather than that the officer induced or encouraged the defendant to engage in a behavior in which s/he would not normally become involved.

SOURCES OF INFORMATION FOR LEGAL RESEARCH

Legal research involves the study of both statutes and case law from court decisions. Because the law is constantly changing, it is essential that only the most recent references be used. Today, much of the material may be found in electronic format: CD-ROMs and online computer databases such as WestLaw and Lexis have significantly streamlined legal research.

Legal Citations

Decisions of state appellate courts and the U.S. Supreme Court are published in books which are generally known as **reports** or **reporters**. A sample case citation is: ***Commonwealth v. Harris,*** **550 Pa. 92 (1997).** This particular case discussed the use of self defense. *Commonwealth v Harris* is the name of the case; all cases heard in Pennsylvania courts are prosecuted as the Commonwealth (of Pennsylvania) versus the name of the defendant. The first number (550) represents the volume number in which the case is to be found. "Pa" is an abbreviation for the specific reporter in which the case is to be found (*Pennsylvania State Reports*). The second number (92) is the page number in the reporter on which the decision is to be found. The date in parentheses (1997) is the year in which the case was decided. Therefore, the above citation, 550 Pa. 92, which was decided in 1997, is found beginning on page 92 of volume 550 of the *Pennsylvania State Reports.*

Statutory citations resemble case citations. A sample statutory citation is: **18 Pa.C.S. §2501**. Pa.C.S. is an abbreviation for the Pennsylvania Consolidated Statutes. The first number (18) refers to the Title of the Consolidated Statutes (in this case Crimes and Offenses) and the second number (2501) refers to the specific section number of the statute. This particular statute deals with the topic of criminal homicide. In some cases, a statutory citation may be in the form **Pa.C.S.A.**, which is an abbreviation for the Annotated Consolidated Statutes. If the citation is to an uncodified or unconsolidated statute, the reference will be in the form **P.S.**, referring to Purdon's Statutes.

Court decisions are found in the following sources:

- ***United States Reports*** (US) – contains U.S. Supreme Court decisions.

- ***Supreme Court Reporter*** (S.Ct) – contains U.S. Supreme Court decisions.

- ***Atlantic Reporter, 2nd series*** (A.2d) – contains decisions from courts in nine states, as well as the District of Columbia. Cases from the Supreme Court, the Superior Court, and the Commonwealth Court of Pennsylvania are published, although cases from the Courts of Common Pleas are not included in the Atlantic Reporter.

- ***Pennsylvania State Reports*** (Pa) – contains the same information as is found in the Atlantic Reporter 2nd series.

- ***Pennsylvania Superior Court Reports*** (Pa. Super.) – the official court reports for the Superior Court of Pennsylvania from 1895 through 1997 (cases after 1997 are found in the Atlantic Reporter 2nd series).

- ***Pennsylvania Commonwealth Court Reports*** (Pa. Commw.) – the official court reports for the Commonwealth Court of Pennsylvania from

1970 through 1995 (cases after 1997 are found in the Atlantic Reporter 2nd series).

- *Pennsylvania District and County Court Reports* (D&C) – includes selected decisions from various Courts of Common Pleas.

- In addition, many counties have their own case reporters. For example, the *Philadelphia Reports*, the *Bucks County Reports*, and so on.

Shepard's Citations

There are two Shepard's Citators reporting Pennsylvania case law, *Shepard's Pennsylvania Citations* and *Shepard's Atlantic Reporter Citations*. Both are available on CD-Rom and contain analyses of appellate court decisions. Each citation includes a history of the case, other decisions which cite this decision, and any other cases which have modified, overruled, or approved the decision.

Other Sources of Information

There are a number of other sources of information on Pennsylvania law. However, it is important to remember that these sources are not official legal authorities.

A **legal digest** is a research tool that arranges issues by topic for easy reference. It allows a researcher studying a legal point from one case to easily find other court decisions which were made on similar issues. *West's Pennsylvania Digest, 2nd series* is one of the most popular legal digests for Pennsylvania. It indexes Pennsylvania's reported cases by both case name and subject. *West's Atlantic Reporter Digest, 2nd series* indexes appellate court cases in all state courts covered by the Atlantic Reporter, 2nd series. It includes the Supreme, Superior, and Commonwealth Courts of Pennsylvania.

Black's Law Dictionary is the most popular **legal dictionary** in America today and can be found in any law library. There are also several useful **legal encyclopedias** which discuss Pennsylvania state law and state legal issues. One of the most popular is *Pennsylvania Law Encyclopedia*, which is an encyclopedia of Pennsylvania substantive and procedural law.

Law reviews are journals which contain scholarly legal research articles written by lawyers and law students. All the major law schools in Pennsylvania publish law reviews. Some of the major law reviews available in Pennsylvania include:

- *University of Pennsylvania Law Review* (U.Pa.L.Rev.)

- *University of Pittsburgh Law Review* (U.Pitt.L.Rev.)

- *Villanova Law Review* (V.L.R.)

- *Temple Law Review* (T.L.R.)

Law review articles are cited in the same way as court cases. For example, **152 U.Pa.L.Rev. 1181** would refer to an article beginning on page 1181 of volume 152 of the *University of Pennsylvania Law Review.* This particular article deals with the issue of double jeopardy in the juvenile justice system. In some cases, articles written by noted legal scholars (as opposed to those written by law schools) may be cited as a persuasive legal authority.

NOTES

1. *The Pennsylvania Manual*, volume 116
    (http://www.dgs.state.pa.us/pamanual/site/default.asp)
2. The Constitution of Pennsylvania may be viewed online in Section 2 of *The Pennsylvania Manual*
3. Pennsylvania House of Representatives. *Creating a Commonwealth: A guide to your state government.* Available online at:
    http://www.legis.state.pa.us/WU01/VC/visitor_info/creating/creating.htm
4. *Ibid*
5. The Constitution of Pennsylvania, Article IV, Section 1
6. The Constitution of Pennsylvania, Article IV, Section 3 *et seq.*
7. The Constitution of Pennsylvania, Article IV, Section 5
8. The Constitution of Pennsylvania, Article IV, Section 6
9. Pennsylvania House of Representatives. *Creating a Commonwealth: A guide to your state government, op cit.*
10. The Constitution of Pennsylvania, Article IV, Section 2
11. The Constitution of Pennsylvania, Article IV, Section 9
12. The Constitution of Pennsylvania, Article II, Section 3
13. The Constitution of Pennsylvania, Article II, Section 5
14. The Constitution of Pennsylvania, Article II, Section 7
15. The Constitution of Pennsylvania, Article II, Section 9
16. The Constitution of Pennsylvania, Article II, Section 10
17. The Constitution of Pennsylvania, Article II, Section 4
18. Pennsylvania House of Representatives. *Creating a Commonwealth: A guide to your state government, op cit.*
19. The Constitution of Pennsylvania, Article V, Section 12
20. Pennsylvania House of Representatives. *Creating a Commonwealth: A guide to your state government, op cit.*
21. *Ibid*
22. *Ibid*
23. *Ibid*

24.   *Ibid*
25.   *Ibid*
26.   The Pennsylvania General Assembly web site (http://www.legis.state.pa.us/)
27.   18 Pa.C.S. §107
28.   18 Pa.C.S. §2502
29.   18 Pa.C.S. §106(a) *et seq.*
30.   18 Pa.C.S. §106(c)
31.   18 Pa.C.S. §106(b)(5)
32.   18 Pa.C.S. §106(b)(9)
33.   18 Pa.C.S. §106(d)
34.   See e.g., *Commonwealth v. Weinder*, 395 Pa.Super. 608, 577 A.2d 1364 (1990)
35.   *Commonwealth v. Roxberry*, 529 Pa. 160, 602 A.2d 826 (1992)
36.   18 Pa.C.S. §503(a)
37.   18 Pa.C.S. §501
38.   18 Pa.C.S. §505(b)(2)
39.   18 Pa.C.S. §505(b)(2)(ii)(A)
40.   *Commonwealth v. Harris*, 550 Pa. 92, 703 A.2d 441 (1997), cert. Denied 525 U.S. 1015, 119
       S.Ct. 538, 142 L.Ed.2d 447 (1998)
41.   18 Pa.C.S. §506
42.   18 Pa.C.S. §311(c)
43.   18 Pa.C.S. §315(a)
44.   18 Pa.C.S. §315(b)
45.   *Commonwealth v. Weinstein*, 499 Pa. 106, 451 A.2d 1344 (1982)
46.   18 Pa.C.S. §314(c)
47.   42 Pa.C.S. §9727
48.   See e.g., *Commonwealth v. Bridge*, 495 Pa. 568, 435 A.2d 151 (1981)
49.   18 Pa.C.S. §309
50.   18 Pa.C.S. §313(a)
51.   18 Pa.C.S. §313(b)

CHAPTER 3

INDEX CRIMES

INTRODUCTION

The Federal Bureau of Investigation (FBI) annually publishes the *Uniform Crime Reports* (UCR)[1], which is the most widely used source of official data on crime and criminals in the United States. Much of the UCR deals with **index crimes**, a set of eight serious offenses that the FBI uses as a measure of crime in the United States. They are also known as **Part 1 Offenses** and include four violent crimes and four property crimes. The eight index crimes measured by the FBI are:

- homicide
- forcible rape
- robbery
- aggravated assault
- burglary
- larceny-theft
- motor vehicle theft
- arson

However, the definitions used by the FBI in compiling the UCR are not always the same as those found in the Pennsylvania Consolidated Statutes. This chapter will discuss the definitions of these eight serious crimes as provided by the Pennsylvania Crimes Code. A discussion of hate crimes in Pennsylvania is also included in this chapter.

CRIMINAL HOMICIDE

Homicide is the killing of one human being by another. If that killing is illegal, then it is a form of **criminal homicide**. The UCR includes the crimes of murder and nonnegligent manslaughter, which are defined as "the wilful (nonnegligent) killing of one human being by another."[2] In Pennsylvania, criminal homicide is discussed in Chapter 25 of the Crimes Code, which states that:

> A person is guilty of criminal homicide if he intentionally, knowingly, recklessly, or negligently causes the death of another person.[3]

Criminal homicide includes the crimes of:

- murder (including first degree, second degree, and third degree)
- manslaughter (voluntary and involuntary)

- homicide by vehicle or watercraft

In addition, Pennsylvania recognizes several categories of non-criminal homicide, including justifiable and excusable homicide.

The basic definition of criminal homicide given in the statutes includes two key elements:

- conduct that causes the death of a person (*actus reus* – the guilty act)

- the mental culpability of the defendant (*mens rea* – the guilty mind)

The specific homicide offense of which a defendant may be convicted depends on his or her level of mental culpability and on the nature of the circumstances surrounding the death (e.g., the presence of aggravating factors).

First Degree Murder

First degree murder is defined in 18 Pa.C.S. §2502, which states that "A criminal homicide constitutes murder of the first degree when it is committed by an intentional killing." The term "intentional killing" is defined by statute as, "Killing by means of poison, or by lying in wait, or by any other kind of willful, deliberate and premeditated killing."[4]

Essentially, the statute identifies three types of first degree murder. The first two, killing by means of poison and killing by lying in wait, are identified by the way the killing was carried out. The third type, however, is established by evidence of **specific intent to kill**, which is the term used by the courts to identify the state of mind required for the crime to be committed willfully, deliberately, and with premeditation. The Pennsylvania Supreme Court has held that:

> ...a murder is wilful, deliberate, and premeditated if it is committed by one who is conscious of his own purpose and intends to end the life of his victim.[5]

Specific intent may be proved by circumstantial evidence, or inferred from the words or actions of the defendant. For example, the state Supreme Court has repeatedly stated that the use of a deadly weapon (such as a gun or knife) on the victim provides inferential evidence of the offender's specific intent to kill the victim.[6]

The law does not define the actual amount of time that must pass between forming the premeditated idea of killing and the actual killing itself. It merely requires that the specific intent to kill be formed consciously before the killing takes place. The courts also have not identified a specific length of time required for an offender to form the required specific intent. However, case law does suggest that the requisite length of time may be extremely brief, minutes or even seconds.[7]

Murder in the first degree is a capital crime in Pennsylvania. According to 18 Pa.C.S. §1102, "A person who has been convicted of a murder of the first degree shall be sentenced to death or to a term of life imprisonment..." 42 Pa.C.S. §9711 discusses the procedures for determining the sentence in a capital crime. After the defendant has been found guilty of murder in the first degree, a separate sentencing hearing shall be held before the same jury to determine whether the sentence will be death or life imprisonment. If the defendant pled guilty or waived his or her right to a jury trial, a jury will be impaneled for the sentencing proceeding. If the defendant waived his or her right to a sentencing jury, the sentence will be determined by the trial judge.

The jury hears evidence relating to possible aggravating and mitigating circumstances, as well as information about the victim and the impact that the victim's death had on the family of the victim. The jury then renders a sentencing verdict to the court, which must impose the sentence which was handed down by the jury. The jury must impose a sentence of death if they find at least one aggravating circumstance and no mitigating circumstances, or if the aggravating circumstances outweigh the mitigating circumstances. In all other situations, the jury must impose a verdict of life imprisonment. Any sentence of death is subject to automatic review by the Supreme Court of Pennsylvania.

Capital punishment in Pennsylvania is discussed in more detail in Chapter 7.

Second Degree Murder

Second degree murder is defined as:

> A criminal homicide constitutes murder of the second degree when it is committed while defendant was engaged as a principal or an accomplice in the perpetration of a felony.[8]

The term "perpetration of a felony" has been defined by statute as involving the commission or attempted commission of the crimes of robbery, rape, deviate sexual intercourse by force or threat of force, arson, burglary, and kidnapping.[9] Essentially, second degree murder in Pennsylvania is **felony murder** and involvement in the underlying felony is an element of the crime, although it is not necessary that the defendant be charged separately with the underlying felony.[10] However, if the killing occurs first and the underlying felony is committed as an afterthought, rather than having been intended from the start, the element is not proven. Therefore, if the offender murders the victim and only then decides to steal the victim's wallet, the offender is not guilty of felony murder.[11]

According to the Pennsylvania Superior Court, there is no crime of attempted second degree murder, because the murder was the unintended result of the felonious act committed by the offender.[12]

Third Degree Murder

According to 18 Pa.C.S. §2502(c), "All other kinds of murder shall be murder of the third degree. Murder of the third degree is a felony of the first degree." Essentially, any murder that does not meet the criteria for first or second degree murder is classified as **third degree murder**. Third degree murder does not require the specific intent to kill, but it does require **malice** or **malice aforethought**, which is the key factor differentiating murder from manslaughter. According to the Pennsylvania Supreme Court,

> ...Malice in its legal sense exists not only where there is a particular ill will, but also whenever there is a wickedness of disposition, hardness of heart, wanton conduct, cruelty, recklessness of consequences and a mind regardless of social duty. Legal malice may be inferred from the attending circumstances ... If there was an unlawful killing with ... malice, express or implied, that will constitute murder even though there was no intent to injure or kill the particular person who was killed and even though his death was unintentional or accidental...[13]

For an offender to be convicted of this crime, malice must be proven. However, not every death that occurred during a fist fight is a case of third degree murder. For example, the case of *Commonwealth v. Thomas*[14] involved a defendant who hit the victim in the head one time. The victim was knocked to the ground, hitting his head on the pavement, and died from the resultant head injuries. The Court found that this death, which was the result of only one blow, did not support the inference of legal malice.

Third degree murder may involve specific intent to harm the victim, as long as it does not involve specific intent to kill, but this intent is not a necessary element of the crime.[15]

Manslaughter

Pennsylvania recognizes two types of **manslaughter**. **Voluntary manslaughter**, a first degree felony, is discussed in 18 Pa.C.S. §2503(a), which states that:

> A person who kills an individual without lawful justification commits voluntary manslaughter if at the time of the killing he is acting under a sudden and intense passion resulting from serious provocation by:
> (1) the individual killed; or
> (2) another whom the actor endeavors to kill, but to negligently or accidently causes the death of the individual killed.

"Serious provocation" has been defined as "Conduct sufficient to excite an intense passion in a reasonable person."[16]

Voluntary manslaughter does not require the existence of legal malice, which is what differentiates this crime from that of murder.[17] The provocation has created a passion that makes it impossible to have legal malice. The courts have not defined what constitutes sufficient provocation to create the passion necessary to negate malice. However, in general, the courts have held that if a "cooling off" period exists between the provocation and the killing, sudden passion did not exist. For example, in the case of *Commonwealth v. Lester*, the victim asked the defendant to move out of her apartment. The defendant claimed that this event created the sudden and intense passion; however, as the murder did not occur until several days later, the court did not agree.[18]

The Crimes Code also identifies a second type of voluntary manslaughter, stating that:

> A person who intentionally or knowingly kills an individual commits voluntary manslaughter if at the time of the killing he believes the circumstances to be such that, if they existed, would justify the killing under Chapter 5 of this title, but his belief is unreasonable.[19]

Chapter 5 of the Crimes Code discusses general principles of justification. This generally involves situations where the defendant used deadly force in self defense, based on an unreasonable (rather than a reasonable) belief that such force was necessary to save the defendant's life. The defendant is attempting to establish an "imperfect" self defense claim and reduce the seriousness of the crime from murder to manslaughter by claiming that at the time of the crime s/he mistakenly believed that the use of deadly force was justified.

Involuntary manslaughter is defined as:

> A person is guilty of involuntary manslaughter when as a direct result of the doing of an unlawful act in a reckless or grossly negligent manner, or the doing of a lawful act in a reckless or grossly negligent manner, he causes the death of another person.[20]

Involuntary manslaughter may include not only acts but also the failure to act if the defendant had a legal duty to act. Therefore, a parent who neglects to provide necessary medical care for a child may be guilty of involuntary manslaughter if the neglect results in the death of the child.[21]

The statutes have not defined what constitutes gross negligence. The courts have held that there is a difference, albeit a very small one, between ordinary and gross negligence. For example, the Pennsylvania Superior Court held that a simple violation of the vehicle code, without any aggravating circumstances, is not sufficient to sustain a conviction of involuntary manslaughter.[22] However, the term "aggravating circumstances" is open to interpretation by the courts and has created some controversy. For example, in *Commonwealth v. Cienkowski*, the Superior Court held that criminal negligence was not present in a death resulting from a collision that occurred because the defendant ran a red light.[23] However, in another case the court ruled that a collision occurring because a driver failed to yield to oncoming traffic while making a left turn did involve criminal negligence.[24]

In most cases, involuntary manslaughter is a first degree misdemeanor. However, if the victim is under the age of 12 and is in the care or custody of the person causing the death, the crime is a second degree felony.[25]

Homicide by Vehicle and Homicide by Watercraft

The Pennsylvania Vehicle Code includes a statute defining the crime of **homicide by vehicle**. According to 75 Pa.C.S. 3732(a)

> Any person who recklessly or with gross negligence causes the death of another person while engaged in the violation of any law of this Commonwealth or municipal ordinance applying to the operation or use of a vehicle or to the regulation of traffic except section 3802 (relating to driving under influence of alcohol or controlled substance) is guilty of homicide by vehicle, a felony of the third degree, when the violation is the cause of death.

The required intent is that the defendant caused the death recklessly or with gross negligence. This requirement was changed in 2000 to conform to the intent element in the definition of involuntary manslaughter. Prior to that time, the intent element was to cause the death "unintentionally."

If the offender was driving under the influence of alcohol or a controlled substance, the crime is **homicide by vehicle while driving under influence**. This crime is a second degree felony and the statute prescribes a mandatory minimum sentence of three years be imposed for each victim, the sentences to be served consecutively.[26]

The crime of **homicide by watercraft** is found in the Fish and Boat Code. This crime is defined in 30 Pa.C.S. §5502.2, which states that:

> Any person who unintentionally causes the death of another person while engaged in the violation of any provision of this title or regulation promulgated under this title applying to the operation or equipment of boats or watercraft, except section 5502 (relating to operating watercraft under influence of alcohol or controlled substance) commits homicide by watercraft, a misdemeanor of the first degree, when the violation is the cause of death.

The intent element for this crime has not been changed to conform to that found in the involuntary manslaughter definition.

If the defendant was under the influence of alcohol or a controlled substance, the crime is **homicide by watercraft while operating under influence**. This crime is a third degree felony and the statute prescribes a mandatory minimum sentence of three years.[27]

Non-Criminal Homicide

Although the UCR focuses specifically on criminal homicide, there are situations when the killing of one human being by another is lawful and therefore not a crime. Non-criminal homicides may be justifiable or excusable.

Excusable homicide is a death that is caused by an accident or other misfortune, when no unlawful intent is involved in the act that caused the death. In Pennsylvania, this is known as **homicide by misadventure**, and includes the accidental killing of another person during the commission of a lawful act. The crime has three elements:

1. The act that resulted in the death must be one that is lawful to perform.

2. The act must have been performed with reasonable care and due regard for others

3. The killing must be accident (not intentional), without lawful intent, without evil intentions on the part of the actor.

All three elements are required to absolve the actor of guilt.[28] An automobile accident that does not involve negligence or any unlawful act on the part of the driver is an example of excusable homicide.

Justifiable homicide is a killing that was committed with the use of justifiable deadly force, generally in self defense or in the defense of another. Because justifiable and excusable homicides are not criminal acts, there are no punishments associated with these acts.

RAPE

In the Uniform Crime Reporting Program, **forcible rape** is defined as "the carnal knowledge of a female forcibly and against her will."[29] In Pennsylvania, the crime of rape is defined as:

> A person commits a felony of the first degree when he or she engages in sexual intercourse with a complainant:
> 1. By forcible compulsion.
> 2. By threat of forcible compulsion that would prevent resistance by a person of reasonable resolution.
> 3. Who is unconscious or where the person knows that the complainant is unaware that the sexual intercourse is occurring.
> 4. Where the person has substantially impaired the complainant's power to appraise or control his or her conduct by administering or employing, without the knowledge of the complainant, drugs, intoxicants or other means for the purpose of preventing resistance.
> 5. Who suffers from a mental disability which renders the complainant incapable of consent.[30]

Sexual intercourse is defined in 18 Pa.C.S. §3101 and requires actual oral, vaginal, or anal penetration. The statute clearly states that the crime of rape is gender neutral so either a male or a female may be convicted of rape.

Essentially, rape involves any sexual intercourse that occurs when the victim is unable to **consent** for one of the reasons given in the statute. If the intercourse occurs because of the presence or threat of forcible compulsion, it is clearly non-consensual. **Forcible compulsion** includes any express or implied physical, emotional, psychological, intellectual, or moral force.[31] It requires more than simple lack of consent; some type of force must be used to compel the victim to engage in sexual intercourse against his or her will.[32] The victim may also fail to consent because s/he is unconscious or lacks conscious awareness of the intercourse. This includes situations in which the offender engages in sexual intercourse with a sleeping victim.[33] Lack of consent may also occur due to some mental deficiency or disability on the part of the victim. In addition, if the victim becomes intoxicated involuntarily or unknowingly, s/he is deemed to be unable to consent.

Rape is a first degree felony. According to subsection (b) of the statute:

> In addition to the penalty provided for by subsection (a), a person may be sentenced to an additional term not to exceed ten years' confinement and an additional amount not to exceed $100,000 where the person engages in sexual intercourse with a complainant and has substantially impaired the complainant's power to appraise or control his or her conduct by administering or employing, without the knowledge of the complainant, any substance for the purpose of preventing resistance through the inducement of euphoria, memory loss and any other effect of this substance.[34]

Therefore, the use of a "date rape drug" increases the statutory penalty for the crime.

If the offender engages in sexual intercourse with a victim under the age of 13, the crime is known as **rape of a child**.[35] If the child suffers serious bodily injury during the offense, the crime is the **rape of a child with serious bodily injury**.[36] Both crimes are first degree felonies. The rape of a child is punishable by imprisonment for up to 40 years, while the rape of a child with serious bodily injury is punishable by a maximum term of imprisonment for life.[37]

In addition to rape, Pennsylvania also recognizes the crime of **involuntary deviate sexual intercourse**, which involves:

> A person commits a felony of the first degree when he or she engages in deviate sexual intercourse with a complainant:
> 1. by forcible compulsion;
> 2. by threat of forcible compulsion that would prevent resistance by a person of reasonable resolution;
> 3. who is unconscious or where the person knows that the complainant is unaware that the sexual intercourse is occurring;
> 4. where the person has substantially impaired the complainant's power to appraise or control his or her conduct by administering or employing, without the knowledge of the complainant, drugs, intoxicants or other means for the purpose of preventing resistance;
> 5. who suffers from a mental disability which renders him or her incapable of consent;

6. who is less than 13 years of age; or
7. who is less than 16 years of age and the person is four or more years older than the complainant and the complainant and person are not married to each other.[38]

The main difference between this crime and the crime of rape is that the required behavior for this crime is not intercourse but deviate sexual intercourse, which includes genital or anal penetration with a foreign object. The statute also defines the crimes of **involuntary deviate sexual intercourse with a child** and **involuntary deviate sexual intercourse with a child with serious bodily injury** and prescribes the same penalties as for the corresponding rape offenses.[39]

The crime of **statutory sexual assault** is a strict liability offense involving an offender who is at least four years older than the victim having sexual intercourse with a victim under the age of 16. However, if the participants are married, then the act is not a crime.[40] To prove statutory sexual assault, two elements must be shown: an underage victim and sexual intercourse (including penetration). Unlike the crimes of rape and deviate sexual intercourse, lack of consent is not an element of this crime.[41]

Finally, the crime of **sexual assault** is a second degree felony. This crime involves non-consensual sexual intercourse that does not include any of the situations provided in the rape or deviate sexual intercourse statutes.[42] Sexual assault is a lesser included offense of rape and involuntary deviate sexual intercourse.[43] However, it is distinct from statutory sexual assault.[44]

Because statutory sexual assault and rape are two separate and distinct crimes, it is possible to convict an offender who has sexual intercourse with an underage victim of both offenses if the elements of each crime are proven beyond a reasonable doubt.[45] Similarly, an offender who is acquitted of one offense may still be convicted of the other.[46] In addition, an offender may be convicted of both rape and involuntary deviate sexual intercourse if the elements of both offenses are proven (e.g., if the offender commits two separate and distinct sexual acts upon the same victim).[47]

Prior to 1995, Pennsylvania had a statute criminalizing the crime of **spousal sexual assault**, which involved sexual intercourse or deviate sexual intercourse with one's spouse by force or threat of force, or when the victim was unconscious.[48] The crimes were second degree felonies because the legislature felt that the crime was less serious when the victim was the offender's spouse. However, the statute was repealed in 1995 and existence of a marital relationship between the victim and the offender no longer affects the way the crime is treated by the courts.

ROBBERY

The Uniform Crime Reporting Program defines **robbery** as "the taking or attempting to take anything of value from the care, custody, or control of a person or persons by force or threat of force or violence and/or by putting the victim in fear."[49] In Pennsylvania, 18 Pa.C.S. §3701 defines robbery as:

(a) (1) A person is guilty of robbery if, in the course of committing a theft, he:

    (I) inflicts serious bodily injury upon another;

    (ii) threatens another with or intentionally puts him in fear of immediate serious bodily injury;

    (iii) commits or threatens immediately to commit any felony of the first or second degree;

    (iv) inflicts bodily injury upon another or threatens another with or intentionally puts him in fear of immediate bodily injury; or

    (v) physically takes or removes property from the person of another by force however slight.

(2) An act shall be deemed "in the course of committing a theft" if it occurs in an attempt to commit theft or in flight after the attempt or commission.

(b) Robbery under subsection (a)(1)(iv) is a felony of the second degree; robbery under subsection (a)(1)(v) is a felony of the third degree; otherwise, it is a felony of the first degree.

Essentially, robbery in Pennsylvania has two elements:

(a) The offender must commit or attempt to commit a theft.

(b) The offender must use or threaten the use of force, or must place the victim in fear of immediate injury, or must commit or threaten to commit a first or second degree felony.

This definition presents robbery as a theft in which the property is taken from the victim against the victim's will, using force, threat of force, or creation of fear of injury . This element of force is what distinguishes robbery from theft. Because of the use of force or fear to illegally acquire personal property, Pennsylvania considers robbery to be both a crime against the person and a crime against property.

Actual force or violence is not required in the crime of robbery. A threat that places the victim in fear of immediate is sufficient. The statute does not define the means by which the force is used or fear is imposed. The Supreme Court of Pennsylvania has held that

> the degree of actual force is immaterial, so long as it is sufficient to separate the victim from his property in, or on or about his body. Any injury to the victim, or any struggle to obtain the property, or any resistance on his part which requires a greater counter attack to effect the taking is sufficient. The same is true if the force used, although insufficient to frighten the victim, surprises him into yielding his property.[50]

Because the element of theft is a requirement for the crime of robbery, if no property is actually taken, the defendant cannot be found guilty of robbery. However, according to the Superior Court, the intent to commit a theft is sufficient to meet the required element for a charge of attempted robbery.[51] However, even if it cannot be shown that the defendant took or intended to take property, s/he may be guilty of some other crime, such as assault.

In 1993, Pennsylvania codified the crime of **robbery of motor vehicle**, which is also known as **carjacking**. 18 Pa.C.S. 3702 defines carjacking as:

> A person commits a felony of the first degree if he steals or takes a motor vehicle from another person in the presence of that person or any other person in lawful possession of the motor vehicle.

According to *Commonwealth v. George*, carjacking has three elements:

1. the stealing, taking or exercise of unlawful control over a motor vehicle;
2. from another person in the presence of that person or any other person in lawful possession of the vehicle;
3. the taking must be accomplished by the use of force, intimidation or the inducement of fear in the victim.[52]

The victim does not have to be forced out of the vehicle for the crime to constitute carjacking. As long as the crime occurs in the victim's presence, the necessary element has been met.[53]

ASSAULT

There is often some confusion about the actual meaning of **assault**. In some states, such as California, Illinois, and Florida, assault does not actually involve the infliction of an injury upon another person; it is merely an intentional attempt or threat to cause an injury. In these states, when an injury is actually inflicted, a **battery** has occurred. However, in Pennsylvania, one of the possible elements of assault is the infliction of some type of bodily injury to another person. Thus, there is no crime of battery in Pennsylvania.

Pennsylvania recognizes both simple and aggravated assault, although the Uniform Crime Reporting Program focuses specifically on aggravated assault, which it defines as:

> an unlawful attack by one person upon another for the purpose of inflicting severe or aggravated bodily injury. This type of assault is usually accompanied by the use of a weapon or by means likely to produce death or great bodily harm.[54]

Simple assault in Pennsylvania is defined as:

> A person is guilty of assault if he:
> 1. attempts to cause or intentionally, knowingly or recklessly causes bodily injury to another;
> 2. negligently causes bodily injury to another with a deadly weapon;

3. attempts by physical menace to put another in fear of imminent serious bodily injury; or
4. conceals or attempts to conceal a hypodermic needle one his person and intentionally or knowingly penetrates a law enforcement officer or an officer or an employee of a correctional institution, county jail or prison, detention facility or mental hospital during the course of an arrest or any search of the person.[55]

This statute was recently revised as part of the extensive recodification process. As a result, a number of related offenses were merged, including the crime of attempted assault, which is now included within the assault statute rather than being a separate offense. The fourth provision, relating to assault with a hypodermic needle originally was added to the statute in 2001 and applied only if the victim was a law enforcement officer. The provision was extended to custodial officers and employees in 2002.

According to the Superior Court, there are two distinct ways in which a simple assault may be committed. The first, which involves attempted injury, requires a specific intent to injure a victim, although no such injury may actually occur. The second type, which involves actually inflicting injury upon the victim, may have either specific intent or implied intent (such as reckless actions on the part of the offender that result in injury to the victim).[56] In addition, the court has held that if the offender intended to put the victim in fear of serious bodily injury, and attempted to create such fear, the element is satisfied even if the victim never actually was put in fear. The intent and attempt are sufficient.[57]

In most cases, simple assault is a second degree misdemeanor. However, if the victim is under 12 years of age and the offender is over 21 years of age, the crime is a first degree misdemeanor. If the assault occurred during a fight entered into by mutual consent it is a third degree misdemeanor.[58] The latter is intended to reduce the seriousness of an assault in which the victim may have been the initial aggressor.

Aggravated assault is a felony offense, rather than a misdemeanor. It is defined as:

(a) A person is guilty of aggravated assault if he:
1. attempts to cause serious bodily injury to another, or causes such injury intentionally, knowingly or recklessly under circumstances manifesting extreme indifference to the value of human life;
2. attempts to cause or intentionally, knowingly or recklessly causes serious bodily injury to any of the officers, agents, employees or other persons enumerated in subsection (c) or to an employee of an agency, company or other entity engaged in public transportation, while in the performance of duty;
3. attempts to cause or intentionally or knowingly causes bodily injury to a any of the officers, agents, employees or other persons enumerated in subsection (c), in the performance of duty;
4. attempts to cause or intentionally or knowingly causes bodily injury to another with a deadly weapon;

5.   attempts to cause or intentionally or knowingly causes bodily injury to a teaching staff member, school board member, or other employee, including a student employee, of any elementary or secondary publicly-funded educational institution, any elementary or secondary private school licensed by the Department of Education or any elementary or secondary parochial school while acting in the scope of his or her employment or because of his or her employment relationship to the school;

6.   attempts by physical menace to put any of the officers, agents, employees or other persons enumerated in subsection (c), while in the performance of duty, in fear of imminent serious bodily injury; or

7.   uses tear or noxious gas ... or uses an electric or electronic incapacitation device against any officer, employee or other person enumerated in subsection (c) while acting in the scope of his employment.

(b) Aggravated assault under subsection (a)(1) and (2) is a felony of the first degree. Aggravated assault under subsection (a)(3), (4), (5), (6) and (7) is a felony of the second degree.[59]

The "persons enumerated in subsection (c)" of the statute include a long list of persons working in the public sector, such as public safety employees, correctional employees, persons employed in the court system, teachers, private detectives, social service agency employees, and specified members of the state government (including the executive branch and the members of the General Assembly).

The statute basically identifies a number of aggravating factors that increase the seriousness of the crime from assault to aggravated assault. These include the seriousness of the injury (if the attempted or aggravated injury is serious bodily injury rather than bodily injury), the use of a deadly weapon, and the status of the victim (one of the public officials listed in the statute).

The courts have ruled in a number of cases that the intent of the offender is an important element of the offense. For example, if the offender intended to inflict serious bodily injury, the crime is considered to be aggravated assault even if the victim only suffered bodily injury (as if, for example, the offender shot the victim at close range but the victim suffered only minor injuries).[60] In addition, the courts have held that if the defendant intended to injure a police officer (or some other person listed in subsection (c) of the statute), s/he may be convicted of aggravated assault even if the victim was not a police officer.[61] On the other hand, if the defendant was ignorant of the official status of the victim (if, for example, the officer did not identify himself or herself as a police officer and then uses force against the defendant), the defendant may be considered to have used self defense, which would negate the required intent.[62]

The statutes also identify several other types of assault offenses. **Assault by prisoner**, a second degree felony, involves any assault committed by an individual who is confined in or committed to a local, county, or state detention or correctional facility.[63] If the assault is committed by a prisoner who is under sentence of death or life imprisonment, the crime is known as **assault by life prisoner** and receives the same punishment as the penalty for second degree murder.[64]

Aggravated assault by vehicle while driving under the influence involves causing serious bodily injury while driving under the influence of alcohol or a controlled substance and is a second degree felony.[65] Finally, the **aggravated assault of an unborn child**, a first degree felony, involves the intentional attempt to cause, or the actual infliction of, serious bodily injury to an unborn child.[66]

BURGLARY

In common law, the crime of **burglary** was defined as the breaking and entering of a dwelling at night with intent to commit a felony. Today, the definition of burglary includes structures other than a dwelling place, can occur during the daytime as well as at night, and can involve either an intended felony or misdemeanor. The UCR defines burglary as the "*unlawful entry of a structure to commit a felony or theft.*"[67]

According to 18 Pa.C.S. §3502,

> (a) A person is guilty of burglary if he enters a building or occupied structure, or separately secured or occupied portion thereof, with intent to commit a crime therein, unless the premises are at the time open to the public or the actor is licensed or privileged to enter.
> (b) It is a defense to prosecution for burglary that the building or structure was abandoned.
> (c) Grading. —
>> (1) Except as provided in paragraph 2, burglary is a felony of the first degree.
>> (2) If the building, structure or portion entered is not adapted for overnight accommodation and if no individual is present at the time of entry, burglary is a felony of the second degree.
> (d) A person may not be convicted both for burglary and for the offense which it was his intent to commit after the burglarious entry or for an attempt to commit that offense, unless the additional offense constitutes a felony of the first or second degree.

The crime of burglary requires two separate and distinct types of intent: the intent to unlawfully enter the building or house and the intent to commit a crime inside the structure. Neither intent alone is sufficient to constitute burglary. First, the offender must intend to unlawfully enter the building or house. If the defendant is licensed or privileged to enter, then there is no such intent. Therefore, if the offender commits a crime in a location that is open to the public, such as a bank or store, s/he cannot be found guilty of burglary. However, if the offender legally enters a store and then enters an area of the store that s/he knew was not open to the public (for example, the offender goes through a door clearly marked "Authorized Personnel Only"), s/he may be guilty of burglary. An individual cannot be found guilty of burglarizing his or her own property, as s/he has the legal right to enter the premises.[68] Secondly, the offender must intend to commit a crime within the structure after the unlawful entry. The intent to commit a crime within the structure must have been formed upon entry, not after entry was completed.[69] If the offender originally entered the structure without the intent to commit any further illegal act (other than the unlawful entry), and only decided to commit an additional crime after entering the premises, s/he may not be convicted of burglary. The crime is completed when the offender enters the building, regardless of whether the offense s/he intended to commit within the structure was actually carried out.

While the crime requires entry, forcible entry or "breaking" is not required. Any form of entry with intent is enough to meet the element of entry required for the crime of burglary. Entry occurs when any part of the offender's body, no matter how slight, is inside the building.[70] The offender's mere presence just outside a door does not constitute entry. However, reaching an arm through a window is sufficient to establish entry because the offender has essentially broken through the boundaries around the building. The statute also states that the offender may use as a defense the fact that the building or structure s/he entered was abandoned. In the case of *Commonwealth v. Henderson*, the Superior Court defined an abandoned building as "one that is wholly forsaken or deserted."[71]

LARCENY-THEFT

The FBI defines **larceny-theft** as:

> the unlawful taking, carrying, leading, or riding away of property from the possession or constructive possession of another. It includes crimes such as shoplifting, pocket-picking, purse-snatching, thefts from motor vehicles, thefts of motor vehicle parts and accessories, bicycle thefts, etc., in which no use of force, violence, or fraud occurs.[72]

In Pennsylvania, the equivalent crime is known simply as **theft** and is discussed in Chapter 39 of the Crimes Code. During the revision of the theft statutes, a number of related offenses were consolidated together, following the approach used by the Model Penal Code. According to 18 Pa.C.S. §3902,

> Conduct denominated theft in this chapter constitutes a single offense. An accusation of theft may be supported by evidence that it was committed in any manner that would be theft under this chapter...

The crime of theft is graded based on the value of the stolen property, the type of property stolen, and the method used to steal the property:

> (a) Theft constitutes a felony of the second degree if:
> (1) The offense is committed during a manmade disaster, a natural disaster or a war-caused disaster and constitutes a violation of section 3921 (relating to theft by unlawful taking or disposition), 3925 (relating to receiving stolen property), 3928 (relating to unauthorized use of automobiles and other vehicles) or 3929 (relating to retail theft).
> (2) The property stolen is a firearm.

(3) In the case of theft by receiving stolen property, the property received, retained or disposed of is a firearm and the receiver is in the business of buying or selling stolen property.

(a.1) Except as provided in subsection (a), theft constitutes a felony of the third degree if the amount involved exceeds $2,000, or if the property stolen is an automobile, airplane, motorcycle, motorboat or other motor-propelled vehicle, or in the case of theft by receiving stolen property, if the receiver is in the business of buying or selling stolen property.

(b) Theft not within subsection (a) or (a.1) of this section, constitutes a misdemeanor of the first degree, except that if the property was not taken from the person or by threat, or in breach of fiduciary obligation, and:

(1) the amount involved was $50 or more but less than $200 the offense constitutes a misdemeanor of the second degree; or

(2) the amount involved was less than $50 the offense constitutes a misdemeanor of the third degree.[73]

The actual value of the property is determined based on the time the crime occurred.

The second section of this chapter discusses a number of specific theft offenses. These include:

1. Theft by unlawful taking or disposition[74]
2. Theft by deception[75]
3. Theft by extortion[76]
4. Theft of property lost, mislaid, or delivered by mistake[77]
5. Receiving stolen property[78]
6. Theft of services[79]
7. Theft by failure to make required disposition of funds received[80]
8. Unauthorized use of automobiles and other vehicles[81]
9. Retail theft[82]
10. Library theft[83]
11. Unlawful possession of retail and library theft instruments[84]
12. Theft of trade secrets[85]
13. Theft of unpublished dramas and musical compositions[86]
14. Theft of leased property[87]
15. Theft from a motor vehicle[88]

An individual who commits any of these offenses is guilty of theft.

MOTOR VEHICLE THEFT

The UCR considers **motor vehicle theft** to be a separate index crime from that of theft or larceny-theft. It is defined by the FBI as:

> the theft or attempted theft of a motor vehicle, this offense category includes the stealing of automobiles, trucks, buses, motorcycles, motorscooters, snowmobiles, etc.[89]

While Pennsylvania does not consider motor vehicle theft to be a separate crime, there are several crimes outlined in the Pennsylvania Statutes which correspond to this index crime. According to 18 Pa.C.S. §3903(a.1), theft is a felony of the third degree if the property stolen is a motor-propelled vehicle (including an automobile or motorcycle). In addition, the crime of **unauthorized use of automobiles and other vehicles**, which is considered to be a theft offense, is defined as:

> A person is guilty of a misdemeanor of the second degree if he operates the automobile, airplane, motorcycle, motorboat, or other motor-propelled vehicle of another without consent of the owner.[90]

This statute includes the crime of **joyriding**, because it does not require that the offender have the intent to permanently deprive the owner of the crime.

In addition, carjacking is defined in 18 Pa.C.S. 3702 (see the discussion under **Robbery** earlier in this chapter) and does involve the taking of a motor vehicle from another's person or custody. In Pennsylvania, carjacking is considered to be a form of robbery rather than a theft.

ARSON

Like burglary, the common-law felony crime of **arson** was a crime against a home or dwelling place. While it could occur at any time of day, nighttime arson was considered to be a more serious crime. The UCR defines arson as:

> any willful or malicious burning or attempt to burn, with or without intent to defraud, a dwelling house, public building, motor vehicle or aircraft, personal property of another, etc.[91]

The Pennsylvania arson statutes were significantly revised in 1982 and Pennsylvania law now recognizes arson against structures other than a home, as well as the burning of other types of property. The crime is divided into five categories, all of which require intent. A fire that is of accidental or unintentional origin is not considered to be arson.

Arson endangering persons is defined by 18 Pa.C.S. §3301(a) as:

(1) A person commits a felony of the first degree if he intentionally starts a fire or causes an explosion, or if he aids, counsels, pays or agrees to pay another to cause a fire or explosion, whether on his own property or on that of another, and if:

    (i) he thereby recklessly places another person in danger of death or bodily injury, including but not limited to a firefighter, police officer or other person actively engaged in fighting the fire; or

    (ii) he commits the act with the purpose of destroying or damaging an inhabited building or occupied structure of another.

(2) A person who commits arson endangering persons is guilty of murder of the second degree if the fire or explosion causes the death of any person, including but not limited to a firefighter, police officer or other person actively engaged in fighting the fire, and is guilty of murder of the first degree if the fire or explosion causes the death of any person and was set with the purpose of causing the death of another person.

Because the life of another person is placed at risk, this type of arson is considered to be the most serious form of the crime.

Arson endangering property involves:

A person commits a felony of the second degree if he intentionally starts a fire or causes an explosion, whether on his own property or that of another, or if he aids, counsels, pays or agrees to pay another to cause a fire or explosion, and if:

    (1) he commits the act with intent of destroying or damaging a building or unoccupied structure of another;

    (2) he thereby recklessly places an inhabited building or occupied structure of another in danger of damage or destruction; or

    (3) he commits the act with intent of destroying or damaging any property, whether his own or of another, to collect insurance for such loss.[92]

This crime includes the burning of any building or structure that does not place another person's life at risk. It also includes the offense of burning to defraud or arson for insurance, which is one of the most common forms of arson. The property involved does not have to be a building or structure; in burning to defraud, the targeted property is often merchandise or other goods.

The third type of arson is known as **reckless burning or exploding**. This is defined in 18 Pa.C.S. §3301(d) and involves:

A person commits a felony of the third degree if he intentionally starts a fire or causes an explosion, or if he aids, counsels, pays or agrees to pay another to cause a fire or explosion, whether on his own property or on that of another, and thereby recklessly:

(1) places an uninhabited building or unoccupied structure of another in danger of damage or destruction; or

(2) places any personal property of another having a value of $5,000 or more in danger of damage or destruction.

The primary difference between this crime and arson endangering property is that this offense does not require the offender have intent to damage or destroy a structure belonging to another. It only requires that the offender recklessly place the structure in danger of damage or destruction.

The offense of **failure to control or report dangerous fires** is a misdemeanor which is defined as:

A person who knows that a fire is endangering the life or property of another and fails to take reasonable measures to put out or control the fire, when he can do so without substantial risk to himself, or to give a prompt fire alarm, commits a misdemeanor of the first degree if:

(1) he knows that he is under an official, contractual or other legal duty to control or combat the fire; or

(2) the fire was started, albeit lawfully, by him or with his assent, or on property in his custody or control.[93]

This offense does not necessarily involve the offender starting a fire. One of the two conditions under which a defendant may be prosecuted merely requires that s/he had a lawful duty to fight or control the fire and fails to fulfill that duty or to report the fire. The other condition involves an offender who started a lawful fire that ends up endangering life or property. An example of this would be a hiker who starts a campfire that gets out of control and who fails to put out the fire or to report it to the authorities.

The final type of arson involves the **possession of explosive or incendiary materials or devices**. This crime is defined in 18 Pa.C.S. §3301(f) as:

A person commits a felony of the third degree if he possesses, manufactures or transports any incendiary or explosive material with the intent to use or to provide such device or material to commit any offense described in subsection (a), (c) or (d).

This is the only type of arson that does not require a fire as an element of the offense. An individual who possesses explosives or incendiary materials may be convicted of this offense without actually starting a fire, as long as s/he has the intent to commit arson endangering persons, arson endangering property, or reckless burning or exploding.

The Pennsylvania arson statutes are significantly different from the common law crime of arson. In Pennsylvania, an individual may be found guilty of arson even if no burning or significant injury occurs. In addition, the courts have held that attempted arson is punishable as severely as the completed offense, because of the risk inherent in the crime. The statutes do not specifically criminalize arson for profit as a separate crime, but they do provide for an additional fine for arson that was committed for profit. The offender will be sentenced to a fine that is twice the amount of the consideration s/he received (or was supposed to receive) for setting the fire, or to the maximum lawful fine, whichever is greater.[94]

HATE CRIMES

Hate or bias crimes are not specifically included among the UCR's eight index crimes. However, the FBI began to collect data on this category of crime after President Bush signed the Hate Crimes Statistics Act in 1990. The UCR defines hate or bias crimes as "those offenses motivated in part or singularly by personal prejudice against others because of a diversity—race, sexual orientation, religion, ethnicity/national origin, or disability.[95]

In Pennsylvania, hate crime is known as **ethnic intimidation**. The crime is defined by 18 Pa.C.S. 2710(a) as any crime against a person, arson, criminal mischief, or any other type of property destruction that is committed "...with malicious intent toward the actual or perceived race, color, religion, national origin, ancestry, mental or physical disability, sexual orientation, gender or gender identity of another individual or group of individuals...." Essentially, if a crime is motivated by hatred or anger toward one of the specified characteristics of the victim, the state considers the crime to be more serious and the offender may be charged with both the offense committed and with the crime of ethnic intimidation. However, for an offender to be convicted of ethnic intimidation, s/he must also be convicted of the underlying offense.[96]

There were a total of 139 hate crimes in Pennsylvania during 2003, targeting 143 victims (several crimes were committed against multiple victims). Of these 139 crimes, 53 percent were crimes against persons, including both assaults and aggravated assaults. Approximately 30 percent of the hate crimes involved vandalism, and 12.5 percent involved disorderly conduct. The most frequent motivation was the race or color of the victim; almost 65 percent of the reported hate crimes were motivated by the victim's race or color. Other motivations included the victim's sexual orientation (18 percent), religion (13 percent), and ethnicity or national origin (5 percent).[97]

An examination of the state's annual *Uniform Crime Reports* shows that the most common motivator for hate crimes is the race of the victim. However, the 2001 data on hate crimes in Pennsylvania showed a significant increase in anti-Muslim (Islamic) hate crimes. This was most likely due to the terrorist attacks on September 11, 2001. In 2002 and 2003, the total number of reported hate crimes returned to pre-2001 levels.

NOTES

1.   Recent issues of the *Uniform Crime Reports* may be viewed online on the Federal Bureau of Investigation's website (http://www.fbi.gov/ucr/ucr.htm)

2. *Ibid*
3. 18 Pa.C.S. §2501
4. 18 Pa.C.S. §2502(d)
5. *Commonwealth v. Stewart*, 461 Pa. 274 279, 336 A.2d 282, 285 (1975)
6. See e.g., *Commonwealth v. Ramos*, 573 Pa. 605, 827 A.2d 1195 (2003)
7. See e.g., *Commonwealth v. Mason*, 559 Pa. 500, 741 A.2d 708 (1999), cert. denied 531 U.S. 829, 121 S.Ct. 81, 148 L.Ed.2d 43 (2000)
8. 18 Pa.C.S. §2502(b)
9. 18 Pa.C.S. §2502(d)
10. See e.g., *Commonwealth v. Munchinski*, 401 Pa.Super. 300, 585 A.2d 417 (1990)
11. *Commonwealth v. Legg*, 491 Pa. 78, 417 A.2d 1152 (1980)
12. *Commonwealth v. Griffin*, 310 Pa.Super. 39, 456 A.2d 171 (1983)
13. *Commonwealth v. Reilly*, 519 Pa. 550, 549 A.2d 503 (1988)
14. *Commonwealth v. Thomas*, 527 Pa. 511, 594 A.2d 300 (1991)
15. *Ibid*
16. 18 Pa.C.S. §2301
17. *Commonwealth v. Hart*, 388 Pa.Super 484, 565 A.2d 1212 (1989)
18. *Commonwealth v. Lester*, 554 Pa. 644, 722 A.2d 997 (1998)
19. 18 Pa.C.S. §2503(b)
20. 18 Pa.C.S. §2504(a)
21. *Commonwealth v. Howard*, 265 Pa. Super. 535, 402 A.2d 674 (1979)
22. *Commonwealth v. Cienkowski*, 290 Pa.Super. 415, 434 A.2d 821 (1981)
23. *Ibid*
24. *Commonwealth v. Setsodi*, 303 Pa.Super. 482, 450 A.2d 29 (1982)
25. 18 Pa.C.S. §2504(b)
26. 75 Pa.C.S. §3735
27. 30 Pa.C.S. §5502.1
28. *Commonwealth v. Musi*, 486 Pa. 102, 404 A.2d 378 (1979)
29. *Uniform Crime Reports, op cit.*
30. 18 Pa.C.S. §3121(a)
31. 18 Pa.C.S. §3101
32. *Commonwealth v. Berkowitz*, 537 Pa. 143, 641 A.2d 1161 (1994); *Commonwealth v. Rhodes*, 510 Pa. 537, 510 A.2d 1217 (1986)
33. See e.g., *Commonwealth v. Price*, 420 Pa.Super 256, 616 A.2d 681 (1992)
34. 18 Pa.C.S. §3121(b)
35. 18 Pa.C.S. §3121(c)
36. 18 Pa.C.S. §3121(d)
37. 18 Pa.C.S. §3121(e)
38. 18 Pa.C.S. §3123(a)
39. 18 Pa.C.S. §3123(b), (c), and (d)
40. 18 Pa.C.S. §3122.1
41. *Commonwealth v. Ruehling*, 232 Pa.Super. 378, 334 A.2d 702 (1975)
42. 18 Pa.C.S. §3124.1

43.   *Commonwealth v. Buffington*, 574 Pa. 29, 828 A.2d 1024 (2003)

44.   *Commonwealth v. Duffy*, 832 A.2d 1132 (Pa.Super. 2003)

45.   *Commonwealth v. Hitchcock*, 523 Pa. 248, 565 A.2d 1159 (1989)

46.   *Commonwealth v. Fulton*, 318 Pa.Super. 470, 465 A.2d 650 (1983)

47.   *Commonwealth v. Hitchcock, op cit.*

48.   18 Pa.C.S. §3128(a), Repealed

49.   *Uniform Crime Reports, op cit.*

50.   *Commonwealth v. Brown*, 506 Pa. 169, 84 A.2d 738 (1984)

51.   *Commonwealth v. Bryant*, 282 Pa.Super. 600, 423 A.2d 407 (1980)

52.   *Commonwealth v. George*, 705 A.2d 916, 920 (Pa.Super. 1998)

53.   *Ibid*

54.   *Uniform Crime Reports, op cit.*

55.   18 Pa.C.S. §2701(a)

56.   *Commonwealth v. Mott*, 372 Pa.Super. 133, 539 A.2d 365 (1988), appeal granted 520 Pa. 603, 553 A.2d 964 (1988)

57.   *Commonwealth v. Repko*, 817 A.2d 549 (Pa.Super. 2003)

58.   18 Pa.C.S. §2701(b)

59.   18 Pa.C.S. §2702(a)

60.   *Commonwealth v. Sirianni*, 286 Pa.Super. 176, 428 A.2d 629 (1981)

61.   *Commonwealth v. Flemings*, 539 Pa. 404, 652 A.2d 1282 (1995)

62.   *Ibid*

63.   18 Pa.C.S. §2703

64.   18 Pa.C.S. §2704

65.   75 Pa.C.S. §3735.1

66.   18 Pa.C.S. §2606

67.   *Uniform Crime Reports, op cit.*

68.   *Commonwealth v. Majeed*, 548 Pa. 48, 694 A.2d 336 91997)

69.   *Commonwealth v. Alston*, 529 Pa. 202, 651 A.2d 1092 (1994)

70.   *Commonwealth v. Rhodes*, 272 Pa.Super. 546, 416 A.2d 1031 (1979)

71.   *Commonwealth v. Henderson*, 278 Pa.Super. 79, 419 A.2d 1366 (1980)

72.   *Uniform Crime Reports, op cit.*

73.   18 Pa.C.S. §3903

74.   18 Pa.C.S. §3921

75.   18 Pa.C.S. §3922

76.   18 Pa.C.S. §3923

77.   18 Pa.C.S. §3924

78.   18 Pa.C.S. §3925

79.   18 Pa.C.S. §3926

80.   18 Pa.C.S. §3927

81.   18 Pa.C.S. §3928

82.   18 Pa.C.S. §3929

83.   18 Pa.C.S. §3929.1

84.   18 Pa.C.S. §3929.2

85.   18 Pa.C.S. §3930

86.   18 Pa.C.S. §3931

87.   18 Pa.C.S. §3932

88.   18 Pa.C.S. §3934

89.   *Uniform Crime Reports, op cit.*

90.   18 Pa.C.S. §3928

91.   *Uniform Crime Reports, op cit.*

92.   18 Pa.C.S. §3301(c)

93.   18 Pa.C.S. §3301(e)

94.   18 Pa.C.S. §3308(a)

95.   Recent issues of the FBI's *Hate Crime Statistics* may be viewed online on the FBI's website (http://www.fbi.gov/ucr/ucr.htm)

96.   *Commonwealth v. Magliocco*, 806 A.2d 1280 (Pa.Super. 2002)

97.   *Crime in Pennsylvania: Annual Uniform Crime Report, 2003.* Available online at: http://164.156.7.189/UCR/Reporting/Annual/AnnualSumArrestUI.asp

CHAPTER 4

THE POLICE IN PENNSYLVANIA

INTRODUCTION

There are many levels of police agencies in America today, including federal law enforcement, state police, county sheriff's agencies, and city police. There are over 1,200 separate law enforcement agencies in Pennsylvania today. Most of these are municipal departments. In addition, there are 67 county sheriff's departments, one state police agency (the Pennsylvania State Police), and a wide variety of special-purpose law enforcement agencies at all levels of government. In 2002, over 25,000 full time sworn law enforcement officers were employed in Pennsylvania. Of these, approximately 89 percent were male and 11 percent were female.[1] However, these statistics are not exact, because approximately one-third of the municipal police departments in the state do not participate in the Uniform Crime Reporting process.[2]

Pennsylvania's location on the East Coast of the United States, and its proximity to both New York and Washington, D.C., creates a number of special law enforcement problems, including issues such as drugs, immigration, and tourism. Because of this, a large number of federal law enforcement agencies have offices in Pennsylvania and/or are involved in law enforcement activities within the state, resulting in a considerable amount of overlap among the various levels of law enforcement in the state.

LOCAL POLICING

The majority of the police departments in Pennsylvania are local or city departments. Every local department is independent of every other department. The goals, purposes, and priorities vary greatly among departments, with each local agency responding to the needs and desires of the population it serves. All municipal police departments are full-service police agencies which provide a wide range of police services, including law enforcement, order maintenance, and service.

According to the Pennsylvania Uniform Crime Reporting System, the largest local police department in the state is the Philadelphia Police Department, with almost 7,000 full-time sworn officers, followed by the Pittsburgh Police Department with almost 900 full-time sworn officers. In contrast, there are a considerable number of local departments with less than five sworn officers.[3]

The Philadelphia Police Department

The **Philadelphia Police Department** (PPD) has existed in some form since the mid-18ᵗʰ century. The City of Philadelphia was established in the 17ᵗʰ century and by 1700 had a population of approximately 4,400. Law enforcement was provided by the Town Watch until 1751, when the city hired wardens and constables to provide limited patrol. In 1850, a police marshal was appointed to supervise the police in the area. The first black officer was hired in 1881 and the first women matron were hired in 1886. Mounted horse patrol began in 1889, motorcycle patrol in 1906, and car patrol in 1936. In 1887, the city created a Department of Public Safety, which included the police department.[4]

Today, the PPD is one of the largest metropolitan police departments in the country, with approximately 6,900 sworn officers in 2002. The department is headed by the Police Commissioner with four Deputy Commissioners supervising different areas of the PPD. **Police Operations** includes most of the "on-street" activities, including the Patrol Bureau, which is divided into six geographic regions, the Detective Bureau, Narcotics Bureau, and Special Operations. The **Administration and Training Division** includes the Training Bureau, which operates the Philadelphia Police Academy, the Administration Bureau, and the Staff Services Bureau. They provide a variety of functions, including human resources, financial planning, budgeting, payroll, and other administrative functions. The **Science and Technology Division** includes the Communications Bureau, which is responsible for the city's 911 operations, Forensic Services, Information Systems, and other special programs. Finally, the **Internal Affairs Bureau** deals with issues involving alleged officer misconduct.[5]

Currently, the minimum entrance requirements for the FLPD include:

- be a U.S. citizen
- have a high school diploma or GED
- be at least 19 years of age but not more than 40 at time of appointment
- have been a resident of Philadelphia for at least one year prior to hiring
- have a valid Pennsylvania drivers license
- no criminal convictions

Applicants who meet these requirements must go through a variety of tests, including a written examination, an oral interview, a background investigation, medical and psychological evaluations, and a physical fitness test. Recruits go through a 40-week, 1,600 hour academy training program, studying a wide variety of subjects including Pennsylvania law, the Pennsylvania motor vehicle code, patrol techniques and procedures, investigations, firearm techniques, defensive techniques, driving training, and first aid. Recruits also go through 160 hours of field training. Base salaries start at $33,861 while in the academy and $36,211 after graduation.[6]

The Derry Township Police Department

The **Derry Township Police Department** (DTPD) provides law enforcement services to Derry Township, which includes Hershey, Pennsylvania. The DTPD is a relatively new department, created in 1966 with three patrol officers and a chief.[7] In 2002, the department employed 42 people, including 36 sworn officers and 6 civilians.[8] In 1997, the DTPD was accredited by the Commission on Accreditation of Law Enforcement Agencies (CALEA). It is only the fifth municipal department in the state to be recognized as an internationally accredited police agency by CALEA.[9]

The DTPT is divided into a number of sections that provide services to the community. The **Patrol Section** is responsible for patrolling the community and responding to all calls for service within Derry Township. Patrol officers also conduct the initial investigation into a crime, before it is referred to a detective for follow-up activities. They are assisted by civilian **Community Service Officers** (CSOs) who do not have arrest powers but may provide help at accident scenes, special events and fires and by directing traffic, dealing with parking enforcement, animal control, and park patrol. The work performed by CSOs frees up sworn officers to handle more serious issues.

The DTPD **Traffic Safety Section** focuses on enforcing traffic laws and dealing with traffic violations such as excessive speeding, driving under the influence, and violations of commercial vehicle laws. The section also conducts traffic and engineering studies and provide a variety of educational programs and materials to members of the public. The detectives working in the **Criminal Investigation Section** investigate serious crimes and cases that require follow-up activities after the patrol officer's preliminary investigation. Within the section are the Forensic Identification Unit, the Drug Investigation Unit, and the Polygraph Unit. Detectives also work closely with the county's Drug Task Force and with local, state, and federal law enforcement agencies. The **Communications Section** operates 24-hours a day and provides police dispatch service for the Township. However, 911 fire and ambulance dispatch service is provided by the Dauphin County Emergency Management Agency Communication Center.[10]

COUNTY POLICING

Each of the 67 counties in Pennsylvania has its own sheriff's department. The Office of the Sheriff was established in the Pennsylvania State Constitution, which states that each county shall elect a sheriff for a term of four years.[11] Sheriffs in Pennsylvania have a wide variety of duties. Today, their primary responsibilities are to the courts. Duties include serving criminal and civil writes, transporting prisoners, providing security for the county courthouse, summoning jurors, making civil arrests, and taking bail in civil cases. In addition, the sheriff is responsible for issuing permits for firearms, for maintaining order during elections, and for executing the judgments of the courts, including conducting sales of real and personal property that has been foreclosed upon by the court. If the office of county coroner is vacant, the sheriff may act in this role as well. Sheriffs have full law enforcement powers and have the authority to enforce criminal and motor vehicle laws throughout the county. Originally, county sheriffs also were in charge of overseeing and running county jails and prisons. However, in most cases, this is no longer a responsibility of the county sheriff.

According to the Bureau of Justice Statistics, as of June 2000, there were a total of 1,719 full-time employees working in county sheriff's offices in Pennsylvania, including 1,428 sworn officers.[12]

The Erie County Sheriff's Office

The **Erie County Sheriff's Office** (ECSO) has been in existence since 1803. The primary functions of the ECSO involve providing service to the courts, focusing on the areas of court security, prisoner custody and transport, and process service. The department is responsible for maintaining order and security in courtrooms and court offices, and for the custody and control of defendants who are incarcerated prior to trial or who have been sentenced by the court. ECSO deputies also transport defendants between the Erie County Courthouse and the Erie County Prison. In 2001, the ECSO transported approximately 4,400 inmates. While awaiting their court appearances, these inmates are housed in the Erie County Sheriff's Holding Facility, which is located in the county courthouse. The facility can house a maximum of 40 inmates at any given time.[13]

The ECSO is divided into eleven divisions, each of which employs both sworn officers and civilians. The **Warrant Division** focuses on enforcing and executing bench warrants. During 2003, over 2,000 warrant files were closed. The division also handles the extradition of fugitives from justice to and from the county. One of the five full-time deputies staffing the division is assigned to the Erie Fugitive Task Force. The **Civil Division** serves court orders, summons, tax liens, writs, subpoenas, and other actions. In 2003, the division served over 6,000 actions. The **Firearms Division** is responsible for processing all applications for licenses to carry firearms, for issuing licenses to qualified applicants, and for licensing firearms dealers in the county. The ECSO issues approximately 2,000 carry licenses annually.[14]

The ECSO **Land Search and Rescue Division** and the **SCUBA Team Division** are made up solely of volunteers. The **Mounted Posse** is also made up of volunteer members, but all members of this division are sworn Special Deputy Sheriffs, rather than civilians. Members of the posse participate in searches and security duties, and each member must maintain his or her own horse and equipment. The Erie County **S.W.A.T. Division** was formed in 1999 and responds to serious and high-risk situations such as hostage rescues, active shooter response, and serving high-risk warrants. All members of the division have volunteered for S.W.A.T duty, have met physical fitness and firearms proficiency requirements, and have completed basic S.W.A.T. training. The **K-9 Division** was founded in 1998. The ECSO is the only department in Erie County to have canines specifically trained in trailing humans and searching for lost or missing persons.[15]

The **School Resource Officer Division** includes four deputies who serve as full-time school resource officers (SRO) in four school districts around the county In addition to implementing a variety of crime prevention measures, the SROs serve as first responders in emergencies. The **Real Estate Division** is responsible for much of the work involved in the sheriff sales. Finally, the **Clerical**

Division prepares all the actions served by the Civil Division, including civil complaints, writs, and summons, as well as scheduling mental health hearings.[16]

Currently, the minimum entrance requirements for a position as deputy sheriff include:

- have a high school diploma
- have two years experience in law enforcement or corrections
- be at least 21 years of age
- have a current valid Pennsylvania driver's license
- have no criminal history
- have no active protection from abuse orders
- be in physical and mental health adequate for the rigorous activity of the job

Prior to applying for the position, applicants must pass an agility test conducted by the department. Applicants who meet the minimum requirements and pass the agility test must take written and psychological examinations, and pass an interview. Selected recruits must attend the Pennsylvania Deputy Training Academy, and pass a 760-hour training program. The starting annual salary for an entry-level deputy sheriff is $23,150.[17]

STATE POLICING

There are two main types of **state police agencies** within the United States. Some states, such as Maryland, operate a **centralized** or full-service state police agency which includes both highway patrol functions and criminal investigation. However, other states, such as North Carolina, separate or **decentralize** the functions and keep criminal investigations separate from the uniformed highway patrol. Pennsylvania uses the centralized system. The main state law enforcement agency is the Pennsylvania State Police.

Pennsylvania State Police

The **Pennsylvania State Police** (PSP) was founded in 1905 in response to a series of labor disputes involving the coal mining industry in the state. The violent **Great Anthracite Strike** of 1902, which led to a national coal shortage, was the final straw that led to the formation of the state agency, which was originally known as the **Pennsylvania State Constabulary**. Business interests supported the creation of the new agency, because the local police were seen as controlled by the working class, and therefore unreliable during labor strikes. However, organized labor movements vigorously protested the new department. The PSP was developed as an extremely military-style agency with statewide general law enforcement powers. The department originally consisted of 228 troopers who were responsible for patrolling the entire state of Pennsylvania.[18]

In 1906, two state troopers were killed in the line of duty. As a result of this incident, the Superintendent of the PSP decided that only single men would be allowed to enlist in the PSP, a ruling that was not rescinded until 1963. The requirement was strengthened in 1927 when the department issued a regulation prohibiting any member of the PSP from getting married without the approval of the Superintendent.[19]

In 1916, the President of the United States, Theodore Roosevelt, spoke about the department, saying that:

> The Pennsylvania State Police is a model of efficiency, a model of honesty, a model of absolute freedom from political contamination. One of the great difficulties in our large States has been to secure an efficient policing of the rural sections. In communities where there are still frontier conditions, such as Texas and Arizona, the need has been partially met by establishing bodies of rangers; but there is no other body so emphatically efficient for modern needs as the Pennsylvania State Police. I have seen them at work. I know personally number of men in ranks. I know some of the officers. I feel so strongly about them that the mere fact a man is honorably discharged from this Force would make me at once, and without hesitation, employ him for any purpose needing courage, prowess, good judgment, loyalty, and entire trustworthiness. This is a good deal to say of any organization, and I say it without qualification of the Pennsylvania Police.[20]

In 1919, the, the size of the PSP was increased to 415 troopers and the agency took over the duties of the State Fire Marshall. That same year, the PSP began motorcycle patrol. In 1920, the **Pennsylvania State Highway Patrol** was created as a separate agency to enforce the motor vehicle laws on state highways. The Highway Patrol was merged with the state police in 1937 and the agency was renamed the **Pennsylvania Motor Police**. In 1943, the department was again renamed the **Pennsylvania State Police**.[21]

In 1954, the first African-American trooper was appointed to the PSP. In 1963, the PSP revoked the requirement that applicants must be single and allowed married men to apply to the agency. In 1971, the department began to accept women as PSP cadets and the first female troopers graduated from the state police academy in 1972. In 1974, the department entered into a consent decree with respect to hiring and promotional practices and procedures, to ensure that the PSP was in compliance with the 1969 Civil Rights Act. In 1993, the PSP gained accreditation from CALEA, the largest police department in the world to become accredited.[22]

The department is headed by a **Commissioner** who has full command and administrative authority over the PSP. A number of offices within the PSP, including the Public Information Office, the Office of the General Counsel, and the Legislative Affairs Office, report directly to the Commissioner. There are three Deputy Commissioners to oversee the daily operations of the PSP. The **Deputy Commissioner of Operations** is responsible for all area commands and for all bureaus performing basic law enforcement operations, including the Bureau of Patrol, the Bureau of Criminal Investigation, the Office of Domestic Security, the Bureau of Drug Law Enforcement, the Bureau of Liquor Control Enforcement, and the Bureau of Emergency and Special Operations. The **Deputy Commissioner of Staff** oversees many of the law-enforcement related staff activities necessary to keep the line officers functioning. These include the Bureau of Forensic Services, the Bureau of Records and Identification, the Bureau of Research and Development, the Bureau of Technology Services, and the Bureau of Staff Services. The **Deputy Commissioner of Administration** oversees the offices and bureaus that keep the PSP running, including the Equal Employment Opportunity Office, the Department Discipline Office.[23]

In 2002, the PSP had a total of 5,589 law enforcement employees. This included 4,410 sworn officers, of which 96 percent were male and 4 percent female, and 1,719 civilian employees, of which 49 percent were male and 51 percent female.[24]

To be eligible to apply for the position of state trooper with the PSP, applicants must meet the following minimum requirements:

- be at least 20 years of age by the date of application
- be at least 21 years of age and less than 41 years of age by the date of appointment as a PSP cadet
- be a resident of the state of Pennsylvania at the time of appointment
- have a valid Pennsylvania driver's license at the time of appointment
- be a U.S. citizen at the time of application
- have a high school diploma or GED as well as 60 semester credit hours or an Associate's Degree at the time of application (the PSP will waive some or all of the credit hour requirement for prior law enforcement experience or military service)

Applicants who meet the minimum requirements must go a series of examinations. Successful completion of each stage of the selection process is required before an applicant may move on to the next state. These include:

- written and oral qualifying examinations
- physical fitness tests (including a 300 meter run, sit-ups, push-ups, a vertical jump, and a 1.5-mile run) and a urinalysis drug screening
- a polygraph examination
- a background investigation conducted by the PSP
- a medical evaluation by the PSP Medical Officer
- a written psychological evaluation

Applicants who successfully complete all phases of the selection process will be eligible for appointment as a cadet.[25]

Cadets are placed on probation for a period of 18 months, and may be dismissed for a variety of reasons, including inefficiency, incompetence, or violating PSP rules and regulations. Cadets attend a 27-week residential academy training program, which includes physical fitness and conditioning, instruction on state law, the state motor vehicle code, weapons training, pursuit driving techniques, first aid and CPR, and participation in a cross-country running program.   After successfully completing the training program, cadets are promoted to troopers and serve the remainder of the probationary period in the field. The starting salary for a trooper is $44,211 per year.[26]

UNIVERSITY AND CAMPUS POLICE

There are a large number of universities in Pennsylvania, each of which has a **campus police force** of some type. University police officers have full law enforcement authority and have the same arrest powers as municipal police officers in or on any property owned, occupied, or used by the college or university.

The University of Pennsylvania is located in Philadelphia and the **University of Pennsylvania Police Department** (UPPD) is the first university police agency in Pennsylvania to receive national accreditation from CALEA. UPPD, which is part of the Division of Public Safety, has 104 sworn officers who are responsible for providing police services to the university. The majority of these officers are assigned to the patrol division, and patrol the campus in patrol cars, on bicycles and motorcycles, and on foot. Officers enforce the law on university property and at university-sponsored events. UPPD also has a detective unit to investigate crimes reported to the police.[27]

Pennsylvania State University has almost two dozen campuses, each of which has a police services agency. The main campus is located in University Park, Pennsylvania. The **University Police** employs 46 full time officers, 6 parking and traffic officers, 5 dispatchers, and approximately 200 student employees. The department patrols the campus, and university-owned properties, on foot, on bicycles, and in patrol cars. The department also enforces parking regulations and handles traffic control on campus.[28]

POLICE TRAINING

Police departments today require highly qualified and well-trained officers. In Pennsylvania, the **Municipal Police Officers' Education and Training Commission** (MPOETC) is under the responsibility of the Pennsylvania State Police.[29] The Commission is made up of 20 members, including the Commissioner of the PSP, the Attorney General of Pennsylvania, the Secretary of Community and Economic Development, and the police commissioner of a city in Pennsylvania. In addition, the Commission includes a member of the Senate and a member of the House of Representatives, and a number of members appointed by the governor. All commission members serve three-year terms.[30]

The MPOETC has a large number of powers and duties specified by statute. These include, but are not limited to:

1. Establishing and administering minimum courses of study for police officers, including basic and in-service training
2. Revoking an officers's certification if s/he fails to comply with training requirements, is convicted of a crime, or is determined by the commission to be physically or mentally unfit to perform his or her duties
3. Establishing minimum qualifications for instructors and approving or revoking approval of any instructor who fails to meet these qualifications
4. Setting minimum standards for physical fitness, psychological evaluation and education as prerequisites to employment as a police officer.
5. Certifying officers who satisfactorily complete the basic educational and training requirements established by the Commission.[31]

The Pennsylvania Code outlines the minimum standards for employment or appointment as a police officer in Pennsylvania. These include the following:

- be at least 18 years of age
- have a high school diploma or a GED
- be a United States citizen
- no criminal convictions
- pass the Nelson-Denny Reading Test at a 9th grade reading level
- be personally examined by a physician licensed in the state of Pennsylvania and be found to meet minimum physical requirements outlined in the statute
- be personally examined by a psychologist licensed in the state of Pennsylvania and be found to be psychologically able to perform the duties of a police officer
- pass a physical fitness evaluation
- pass a background investigation conducted by the employing police agency
- certify whether or not s/he has taken a physical or psychological examinations in conjunction with an application for police employment within the past year and the outcome of the examinations
- successfully complete the basic police training program (unless eligible for a waiver or training under the statute)
- pass the Pennsylvania Officer Certification Examination[32]

The MPOETC has developed a basic recruit training program to provide recruits with the skills required to become certified as Pennsylvania state police officers. Currently, there are 34 municipal police academies that have been certified by the commission.[33] All basic training programs must include the following topics:

1. Pennsylvania criminal law
2. Pennsylvania Rules of Criminal Procedure
3. Pennsylvania Vehicle Code
4. Antisocial behavior
5. Professional relations

6.   Physical conditioning
7.   Human relations skills
8.   Application of force
9.   Firearms training
10.   Patrol procedures and operations
11.   Investigations
12.   Communications
13.   Handling violent and dangerous people
14.   Custody
15.   First aid and CPR
16.   Operation of patrol vehicle
17.   Other subjects the Commission deems necessary[34]

If a recruit completes the minimum requirements for certification, s/he will be certified by the MPOETC for a period of two years. The officer must renew his or her certification every two years, by completing mandatory in-service training.[35] Minimum in-service requirements include annual firearms qualification, maintaining first aid and CPR certifications, and at least twelve hours of annual academic in-service training.[36]

NOTES

1.   *Crime in Pennsylvania: Annual Uniform Crime Report, 2003.* Available online at: http://164.156.7.189/UCR/Reporting/Annual/AnnualSumArrestUI.asp

2.   Wilkerson, James E. (2003, February 23). "State distorts crime statistics: Pennsylvania program doesn't account for unreported incidents." *The Morning Call.* Available online at: http://www.mcall.com/news/local/all-5ucrfeb23.story

3.   *Crime in Pennsylvania: Annual Uniform Crime Report, 2003, op cit.*

4.   Philadelphia Police Department web site (http://www.ppdonline.org/ppd_home.htm)

5.   *Ibid*

6.   *Ibid*

7.   Township of Derry Police Department web site (http://derrycops.com/index.html)

8.   Federal Bureau of Investigation (2003). *Crime in the United States, 2002.* Available online at: http://www.fbi.gov/ucr/02cius.htm

9.   Township of Derry Police Department web site, *op cit.*

10.   *Ibid*

11.   Pennsylvania Constitution, Article IX, Section 4

12.   Reaves, Brian A. and Matthew J. Hickman (2002). *Census of State and Local Law Enforcement Agencies, 2000.* Bureau of Justice Statistics Bulletin, NCJ 194066. Available online at: http://www.ojp.usdoj.gov/bjs/pub/pdf/csllea00.pdf

13.   Erie County Sheriff's Office web site (http://www.eriecountysheriffs.org/)

14.   *Ibid*

15.   *Ibid*

16.   *Ibid*
17.   *Ibid*
18.   Pennsylvania State Police web site (http://www.psp.state.pa.us/)
19.   *Ibid*
20.   *Ibid*
21.   *Ibid*
22.   *Ibid*
23.   Pennsylvania State Police (2004). *2003 Annual Report*. Available online at: http://www.psp.state.pa.us/psp/lib/psp/PSP_Annual_Report_2003.pdf
24.   Federal Bureau of Investigation (2003). *Crime in the United States, 2002, op cit.*
25.   Pennsylvania State Police web site, *op cit.*
26.   *Ibid*
27.   University of Pennsylvania Division of Public Safety web site (http://www.publicsafety.upenn.edu/default.asp)
28.   Penn State University Police web site (http://www.psu.edu/dept/police/)
29.   53 Pa.C.S. §2161
30.   53 Pa.C.S. §2162
31.   53 Pa.C.S. §2164
32.   37 Pa. Code §203.11
33.   Municipal Police Officers' Education and Training Commission (http://www.mpoetc.state.pa.us/mpotrs/site/default.asp)
34.   37 Pa. Code §203.51
35.   37 Pa. Code §203.13
36.   37 Pa. Code § 203.52

CHAPTER 5

THE COURT SYSTEM IN PENNSYLVANIA

The criminal court system in Pennsylvania is a hierarchical system that the state describes as a pyramid. There are two levels of appellate courts and two levels of trial courts. The Pennsylvania Supreme Court is the state's highest appellate court. Below the Supreme Court are the Superior Court, which hears both civil and criminal appeals, and the Commonwealth Court, which hears appeals from decisions by state agencies. Below these are the Courts of Common Pleas, which hear major criminal and civil cases. On the lowest level are the Special Courts.[1]

UNITED STATES DISTRICT COURTS

There are a number of federal courts which sit in Pennsylvania. These are not part of the Pennsylvania state court system and should not be confused with the state trial and appellate courts.

The **U.S. District Courts** are the trial courts of the federal court system. There are three federal judicial districts in Pennsylvania, each with a **federal district court**. These are the:

- Eastern District Court, which serves 9 counties (including Philadelphia)
- Middle District Court, which serves 33 counties
- Western District Court, which serves 25 counties[2]

The **U.S. Courts of Appeals** are the intermediate appellate courts of the federal court system and have appellate jurisdiction only over federal laws. Judges in these courts serve life terms. They are nominated by the President of the United States and confirmed by the Senate. Pennsylvania, along with Delaware, New Jersey, and the Virgin Islands, is part of the Third Circuit.[3]

THE HISTORY OF THE PENNSYLVANIA COURT SYSTEM

The Pennsylvania court system has its roots in the various courts set up during the colonial period by the Duke of York and later by William Penn. There was no "supreme court," as all final appeals were brought before an English court. The Judiciary Act of 1722 established the first court of final appeal in the colony. Although the Act was passed by the colonial legislature in 1722, it did not come into effect until 1727, when it was approved by the English crown. The Judiciary Act established both the Pennsylvania Supreme Court and the Court of Common Pleas. The Supreme Court was made up of three justices, including a chief justice, who sat in Philadelphia twice annually and rode circuit around the state the rest of the year.

In 1776, the Pennsylvania Constitution established several new courts, including the Orphans' Courts and the Courts of Sessions. In addition, the Courts of Common Pleas were expanded to all counties in the new state. The Constitution of 1790 created judicial districts, and in 1895, the Superior Court was created by the General Assembly to serve as an intermediate appellate court and reduce the workload of the Supreme Court.

The Constitution of 1968 created the Commonwealth Court, which was designed to reduce the workload of the Supreme and Superior Courts. The entire court system was reorganized into a **unified judicial system** by this constitution. Twelve years later, in 1980, the legislature reduced the jurisdiction of the Supreme Court, allowing it to focus on cases of key significance to the state and on the administration of the judicial system of the state. To compensate for this, the jurisdiction of the Superior Court was increased simultaneously.[4]

JUSTICES AND JUDGES IN PENNSYLVANIA

All judges and justices in the Pennsylvania court system are required to be citizens of the Commonwealth of Pennsylvania and to meet residency requirements. Judges serving in statewide courts must have been a resident of the Commonwealth for at least one year prior to election or appointment and other judges must have lived within their district for at least one year prior to election or appointment. All judges must live within their jurisdiction (district or statewide) during their time in office. With the exception of Philadelphia traffic court judges and justices of the peace, all judges and justices must be members of the state bar.[5]

All judges and justices in the Unified Judicial System, except special courts judges, are elected to a term of office. Most serve ten-year terms, although justices of the peace and the judges of Philadelphia's Municipal and Traffic Courts serve six-year terms.[6] The judges of the Pittsburgh Magistrates Court are appointed by the mayor of Pittsburgh and serve terms of four years. There is no limit on the number of terms a judge may serve. All judges must retire upon reaching the age of 70, although retired judges are often allowed to serve as senior judges until the age of 75.

THE PENNSYLVANIA SUPREME COURT

The **Pennsylvania Supreme Court** was established in 1722. It is the highest court in the state and is the court of last resort in Pennsylvania. Its decisions are binding upon all other courts in the state. It is made up of seven justices, including a Chief Justice and six associate justices.[7] The Chief Justice is the justice on the Court with the longest continuous record of service. A majority of justices (four) constitute a quorum.[8]

The Supreme Court has general administrative and supervisory authority over all courts in the Commonwealth.[9] The Court's jurisdiction falls into four main categories: original, appellate, exclusive, and extraordinary jurisdiction. The Court has **nonexclusive original jurisdiction** over three types of cases:

- *habeus corpus* - cases in which an individual has been detained and the Court must determine whether the detention occurred without due process.

- *mandamus* - cases that are prohibited to courts of lower jurisdiction.

- *quo warranto* - cases involving a lawsuit which challenges an individual's right to legally hold a public office.[10]

The Court has both discretionary and mandatory **appellate jurisdiction**. Mandatory appeals include final orders from the Courts of Common Pleas, which are specified by statute; the mandatory review of any death sentence is included in the statutory mandate.[11] The Court also hears discretionary appeals from the Superior Court and the Commonwealth Court.[12] The Supreme Court has **exclusive jurisdiction** over appeals from a variety of boards and commissions, including (but not limited to) the Pennsylvania Board of Law Examiners, the Disciplinary Board of the Supreme Court, and the Legislative Reapportionment Commission. Finally, under **extraordinary jurisdiction,** also known as "Kings Bench" powers, the Supreme Court may, in specific situations, assume jurisdiction over a pending case from a court of any level and enter a final order in that case.[13]

PENNSYLVANIA SUPERIOR COURT

The **Pennsylvania Superior Court** is one of the state's two intermediate appellate courts of review.   It was established in 1895 by the General Assembly and originally was made up of seven judges all of whom sat on every case. In 1978 the Supreme Court ordered the Superior Court to sit in panels of three judges. Each panel constitutes a quorum by order of the Supreme Court. The purpose of the change was to allow the Superior Court to better manage the large number of appeals coming to the Court each year. The following year, the state constitution was amended to increase the number of Superior Court judges to fifteen.[14] Although in the past, hearings were conducted by panels made up of judges from the Supreme Court and the Court of Common Pleas as well as from the Superior Court, today all hearings are conducted by panels made up solely of Superior Court judges.

The Superior Court has very limited original jurisdiction. Primarily, the court's original jurisdiction includes applications made under the Wiretapping and Electronic Surveillance Control Act by district attorneys and by the state attorney general. The court has exclusive appellate jurisdiction of appeals from final orders from the Courts of Common Pleas. This includes petitions dealing with a wide variety of issues, including criminal cases, family matters (custody, adoption, divorce, etc.), wills and estates, property disputes, and personal injury cases. In most cases, the Superior Court is the court of final appeal because the Supreme Court denies the majority of petitions for appeal from the Superior Court.[15] There are exceptions of course; if an appeal is within the exclusive jurisdiction of the Supreme Court (e.g., an appeal from a death sentence), then the case will go directly to the Supreme Court and will not be heard by the Superior Court.[16] In 2003, a total of 8,081 appeals were decided by the Superior Court, including 3,504 civil cases and 4,577 criminal cases.[17]

PENNSYLVANIA COMMONWEALTH COURT

The state's second intermediate appellate court is known as the **Commonwealth Court.** It was created by the Constitution of 1968 and has nine justices. It was designed to reduce the workload of the Supreme and Superior Courts by handling some of the appellate cases. The Court also has original jurisdiction over cases brought by and against the Commonwealth of Pennsylvania. Essentially, in cases where the Commonwealth is a party to the case, the Commonwealth Court acts as a trial court of original jurisdiction. These include civil actions that are brought against the government of the Commonwealth of Pennsylvania or against an officer of the government, and civil actions that are brought by the Commonwealth of Pennsylvania.[18]

The appellate jurisdiction of the Commonwealth Court includes appeals from the Courts of Common Pleas in cases involving actions by or against the Commonwealth, various local government matters, and eminent domain proceedings. In addition, appeals from decisions made by state administrative agencies are usually heard in the Commonwealth Court.[19]

PENNSYLVANIA COURTS OF COMMON PLEAS

The Courts of Common Pleas are the state's general trial courts. There is one Court of Common Pleas in each of the 60 judicial districts in the state. Most are single county districts but seven of the judicial districts include two counties. The number of judges in each court varies greatly. Eleven of the judicial districts have only one judge each while the first judicial district (the City and County of Philadelphia) has 93 judges.[20] Each district has a president judge. If the district has at least 8 judges, the president judge is elected by the judges in the district to a term of 5 years. In districts with less than eight judges, the president judge is the judge with the longest period of continuous service.[21]

Common Pleas Courts have original jurisdiction over all major civil and criminal cases, most cases involving families and children, and any other cases that have not been assigned to another court. In addition, they have appellate jurisdiction over appeals from the Special Courts, some state government agencies, and most local government agencies.[22]

In several of the larger counties, the Pennsylvania Consolidated Statutes has mandated that the Court of Common Pleas be divided up into several divisions.[23] For example, in Philadelphia County, there are three separate divisions: the Trial Division has 67 judges, the Family Court Division has 20 judges, and the Orphans' Court Division has 3 judges. Judges are assigned to a division by the president judge.[24]

PENNSYLVANIA SPECIAL COURTS

The lowest level of the Unified Judicial System is made up of a variety of **special** or **minor courts**. These include district justice courts, the Pittsburgh Magistrates Court, the Philadelphia Municipal Court, and the Philadelphia Traffic Court. Special courts are responsible for hearing traffic cases and less serious civil and criminal cases. They also preside over bail hearings and decide whether there is sufficient probable cause for serious criminal cases to be heard by the Court of Common Pleas.

District Justice Courts

District justice courts exist in all counties in Pennsylvania except Philadelphia. District justices issue arrest warrants, preside over preliminary arraignments and preliminary hearings, and fix and accept bail in all criminal cases other than murder or voluntary manslaughter. They also may conduct nonjury trials concerning certain civil claims of up to $8,000.[25]

Unlike judges in higher courts, district justices do not have to be members of the state bar. However, justices who are not lawyers must complete a course of instruction in their duties and responsibilities and must and pass a qualifying exam before being allowed to serve.[26]

Pittsburgh Magistrates Court

The **Pittsburgh Magistrates Court** is made up of six police magistrates who are members of the state bar. They are appointed by the mayor of the city and serve four-year terms. The Pittsburgh Magistrates Court is the only court in the state where judges are appointed rather than elected.[27]

The Magistrates Court is divided into three separate sections: City Court, Traffic Court, and Housing Court. The **City Court** is responsible for arraignments and preliminary hearings in both felony and misdemeanor criminal cases to determine whether there is probable cause to send the case to the Court of Common Pleas. It may also hold trials in summary offenses involving violations of local ordinances. These cases generally involve only fines rather than a punishment of incarceration. The **Traffic Court** handles violations of the state Motor Vehicle Code, parking violations, and charges of driving under the influence. **Housing Court** deals with violations of laws that relate to housing and safety such as the city's building and fire prevention codes and the county health code.[28]

Philadelphia Municipal Court

The **Philadelphia Municipal Court** is one of two special courts of limited jurisdiction in Philadelphia County. It is made up of 25 judges who must be members of the state bar. The Court's **Criminal Division** conducts trials for misdemeanor cases involving offenses that have a maximum sentence of no more than five years incarceration. It also has initial jurisdiction in adult criminal cases and is responsible for holding preliminary hearings in most felony cases to determine whether there is probable cause to send the case to the Court of Common Pleas. The **Civil Division** may hear civil cases involving up to $10,000 in small claims cases and $15,000 in real estate and school tax cases. The division also hears all landlord and tenant cases regardless of the dollar amount in question.[29]

Philadelphia Traffic Court

The second special court of limited jurisdiction in Philadelphia County is the **Philadelphia Traffic Court**. It includes seven elected judges who, like district judges, are not required to be lawyers but must complete a course of education and pass a qualifying examination. The president judge is appointed by the governor. The Court handles offenses covered by the state's Motor Vehicle Code and city traffic ordinances.[30]

COURT ADMINISTRATION

The Administrative Office of Pennsylvania Courts

The Administrative Office of Pennsylvania Courts (AOPC) was created in 1969 after the constitutional convention of 1967-1968 gave the Supreme Court supervisory and administrative authority over all courts in the state. The AOPC carries out these administrative duties and responsibilities. The duties of the AOPC include:

- reviewing practices, procedures and efficiency at all levels of the court system and in all related offices
- developing recommendations to the Supreme Court regarding improvement of the system and related offices
- representing the Judicial System before legislative bodies
- examining administrative and business methods used by offices in or related to the court system
- collecting statistical data
- examining the state of the dockets and making recommendations for expediting litigation
- managing fiscal affairs, including budget preparation, disbursements approval, and goods and services procurement
- supervising all administrative matters relating to offices engaged in clerical functions
- maintaining personnel records

- conducting education programs for system personnel
- receiving and responding to comments from the public
- publishing an annual report
- providing legal services to system personnel.[31]

The Pennsylvania Bar Association

The **Pennsylvania Bar Association** (PBA) was created in 1895 by a group of approximately 200 lawyers from around the state. The association was chartered in July and had 592 charter members. Today, the PBA has over 27,000 members. The mission of the PBA is:

> to advance the science of jurisprudence; to promote the administration of justice; to see that no one, on account of poverty, is denied his or her legal rights; to secure proper legislation; to encourage a thorough legal education; to uphold the honor and dignity of the bar; to cultivate cordial intercourse among the lawyers of Pennsylvania; and to perpetuate the history of the profession and the memory of its members.[32]

The **Pennsylvania Bar Institute** (PBI) provides continuing legal education, including a variety of courses to allow attorneys to earn Continuing Legal Education (CLE) credits. All Pennsylvania lawyers are required to earn twelve CLE credits each year to maintain their legal certification.[33]

The Pennsylvania Board of Law Examiners

The **Pennsylvania Board of Law Examiners** (PBLE) is responsible for admitting individuals to the Pennsylvania bar. The Board reviews applications for admission to the bar from individuals who want to sit the bar exam as well as applications from out-of-state attorneys who want to be admitted to the Pennsylvania bar without sitting the exam. The Board administers the bar exam and makes recommendations to the Supreme Court regarding rules of admission to the bar and rules relating to the practice of law in Pennsylvania.[34]

During the 19th century, each county in Pennsylvania had a separate examining body and an attorney would be licensed to practice law only in the county to which he was admitted. This created administrative difficulties and inconsistencies as each county had different admission standards. In 1902, the Pennsylvania Supreme Court established the PBLE and gave the Board the responsibility for creating a standardized statewide system of bar admissions that did not allow for political influence or geographic discrimination.[35]

The Board currently consists of seven members who are appointed by the Supreme Court and who serve three-year terms. Each member may serve no more than two terms. The bar examination is administered twice each year and lasts two days. The first day includes performance test and six essay questions that have been approved by the Board. On the second day, candidates take the Multistate Bar Examination, which is a nationally standardized test made up of 200 multiple choice questions on six subject areas.[36]

PENNSYLVANIA CRIMINAL COURT PROCEDURES

The basic procedures involved in a criminal trial, including the pretrial activities, are similar in most states. In Pennsylvania, the criminal justice process begins when the police are notified (or in some other way discover) that a crime has been committed and they initiate an investigation into that crime. The procedures discussed in this section apply specifically to felony offenses; however, the procedures for misdemeanors are extremely similar.

Arrest and Booking

After the police have determined both that a crime has in fact been committed and that a specific person committed the crime, they may place that individual under **arrest**. In some situations, the police may have obtained an **arrest warrant** from a court.[37] However, in Pennsylvania, as in most states, many arrests are made by police officers acting without a warrant. A warrantless arrest may be made if the officer has probable cause to believe "there is ongoing conduct that imperils the personal security or endangers public or private property."[38]

Before being brought before a judge, the arrested suspect is taken to the county jail to undergo the **booking** procedure. This involves entering into the police record various facts about the suspect. The suspect will be photographed and fingerprinted and may be placed in a police lineup.

Preliminary Arraignment

In most cases, after being arrested, the defendant must be brought before a district judge as soon as possible for a **preliminary arraignment**. However, there are some exceptions to this. The arresting officer may release the defendant from custody without taking him or her before the court if:

- the most serious charge against the offender is a second degree misdemeanor

- the defendant is a resident of the Commonwealth of Pennsylvania

- the defendant poses no threat of immediate physical harm to anyone (including the defendant)

- the arresting officer has reasonable grounds to believe that the defendant will appear before the court when required

- the defendant does not demand to be brought before the court[39]

However, if all of these conditions are not met, the defendant must be brought before the court as soon as possible.[40]

During the preliminary arraignment, the defendant will be advised of his or her rights and given a written copy of the complaint against him or her. The complaint will also be read to the defendant and a preliminary hearing will be schedule, to be held not less than three or more than ten days after the preliminary arraignment.[41]

If the defendant was not released prior to the arraignment, the arraigning judge will also decide at this time whether the defendant is entitled to any form of **pretrial release**, including **bail**. Although the U.S. Supreme Court stated in *Stack v. Boyle*[42] that the U.S. Constitution does not guarantee the right to bail, the Pennsylvania State Constitution does provide a substantive right to bail in most cases, stating that:

> All prisoners shall be bailable by sufficient sureties, unless for capital offenses or for offenses for which the maximum sentence is life imprisonment or unless no condition or combination of conditions other than imprisonment will reasonably assure the safety of any person and the community when the proof is evident or presumption great; and the privilege of the writ of habeas corpus shall not be suspended, unless when in case of rebellion or invasion the public safety may require it.[43]

There are several types of release on bail, which are discussed in 234 Rule 524. **Release on recognizance** (ROR) involves releasing the defendant without any monetary or property bail. The defendant executes a written agreement to appear in court when required and to comply with the conditions of bail bond which are specified in 234 Rule 526(A). **Release on nonmonetary conditions** also does not require the defendant to provide any monetary or property surety but requires the defendant to comply with nonmonetary conditions specified in 234 Rule 527. These may include travel restrictions, reporting requirements, or other conditions imposed by the court to ensure the defendant's appearance in court. **Release on an unsecured bail bond** requires the defendant to execute a written promise to be liable for a specified amount of money if s/he fails to appear as required or to comply with the conditions of bail bond. However, this type of release does not require the defendant to deposit any money with the court as security. **Release on nominal bail** requires the defendant to deposit a nominal sum (such as one dollar) with the court. In addition, a designated individual or agency agrees to act as surety for the defendant. Finally, **release on a monetary condition** requires the defendant to deposit ten percent of the full amount of the monetary bail with the court in exchange for pretrial release,

When deciding whether or not to release a defendant, and what type of release to employ, the court considers a variety of factors. These include the charge against the defendant, the defendant's employment record, financial resources, family ties, age, character, reputation, history of mental illness (if any), addiction to alcohol or drugs, prior criminal record, prior record of bail release, and any other factors that may be relevant.[44]

Preliminary Hearing

The **preliminary hearing** takes place before a district justice between three and ten days after the preliminary arraignment. At the preliminary hearing, the Commonwealth must prove to the court that there is probable cause to believe that a crime has been committed and that the defendant probably committed that crime. This is known as a *prima facie* case. The defendant may be represented by counsel at the preliminary hearing. If the Commonwealth (usually in the person of the assistant district attorney) is unable to present a *prima facie* case, the defendant will be discharged. If a *prima facie* case is presented, the case will be held for a trial before the Court of Common Pleas.

If the defendant is held for court and did not receive pretrial release at the preliminary arraignment, the district judge may set bail as allowed by law. If the defendant was released at the preliminary arraignment, the judge may continue the existing bail order or modify it.[45]

Filing an Information

If the district judge holds a case for court, the district attorney's office will file an **information**, which is a formal charging document, with the clerk of courts. The information specifies the the charges against the defendant and provides details about the offense the defendant is alleged to have committed.[46] A copy of the information is provided to the defendant upon request.[47]

Formal Arraignment

During the **formal arraignment**, the defendant is formally notified of the charges being brought against him or her. If the defendant has not yet received a copy of the information, a copy will be provided at the arraignment. The defendant is also advised of his or her rights, including the right to counsel and the right to file various pretrial motions. The defendant may waive his or her right to an arraignment if s/he is represented by counsel, the defense counsel agrees with the waiver, and both the defendant and defense counsel sign a waiver of appearance at arraignment form.[48]

The defendant may also enter a **plea** at the arraignment. In most cases, defendants will plead either guilty or not guilty. However, with the consent of the court, a defendant may plead *nolo contendere*, which indicates that, although the defendant is not admitting guilt, s/he does not contest the charges. A judge will not always permit a plea of *nolo contendere*. If a defendant refuses to plead, a plea of not guilty is entered into the record.[49] If a defendant enters a plea of guilty or *nolo contendere* to a felony, s/he waives the right to a trial and the judge may impose a sentence. If a plea of not guilty is entered, the defendant is assigned a date for a pretrial conference and a formal trial.

The Pretrial Conference and Plea Bargaining

In most cases, the defendant, the defense attorney, and the assistant district attorney representing the Commonwealth appear before the assigned judge for a **pretrial conference**. At this meeting, various pretrial matters will be resolved and the parties may discuss a variety of issues. According to the Pennsylvania Criminal Procedure Rules, the topics dealt with at the pretrial conference include:

(1) the terms and procedures for pretrial discovery and inspection;

(2) the simplification or stipulation of factual issues, including admissibility of evidence;

(3) the qualification of exhibits as evidence to avoid unnecessary delay;

(4) the number of witnesses who are to give testimony of a cumulative nature;

(5) the defenses of alibi or insanity, as to which appropriate rulings, may be made; and

(6) such other matters as may aid in the disposition of the proceeding.[50]

While **plea bargaining** is not a formal stage of the criminal justice process, it is an extremely important process in every state, including Pennsylvania. The majority of all felony and misdemeanor convictions in Pennsylvania are the result of guilty pleas. Generally, plea bargaining involves an attempt to resolve or dispose of a case without a trial. During the plea bargaining process, the prosecutor negotiates with the defense attorney (or the defendant), usually at the pretrial conference. In most cases, the purpose or goal of the negotiation is to reach an agreement whereby the defendant will enter a plea of guilty to a charge. This may be the original charge or a lesser or related charge. In exchange for this plea, the prosecutor may do one or more of the following:

- drop other charges which have been filed against the defendant;

- agree to a specific sentence;

- promise to recommend a specific sentence to the court; or

- agree not to oppose the defendant's request for a certain sentence.

The defense attorney is responsible for advising the defendant of all plea offers and any other relevant matters that may affect the defendant's decision, such as the possible results of each plea. The defense attorney may not accept any plea bargain without the full voluntary consent of the defendant. The trial judge does not participate directly in plea bargaining. However, the judge is still an important element in the process because all plea bargains must be approved by the judge. Plea bargaining may continue up to and even during the trial.

Pretrial Motions

A **pretrial motion** is a request that the judge file an order of some type. Pretrial motions may be made by the defense or the prosecution. To save time, Pennsylvania allows all pretrial motions for relief to be included in an **omnibus pretrial motion**, which must be filed and served within thirty days after arraignment.[51] Motions that may be included in such an omnibus motion include a request for::

- a continuance
- suppression of evidence

- a psychiatric examination
- a change of venue
- a change of venire
- a pretrial conference

Discovery

During the pretrial **discovery** process, the defense and the prosecution have the opportunity to obtain additional information about the opponents' cases and to inspect documents and physical evidence. The discovery process is discussed in detail in Rule 573 of the Pennsylvania Criminal Procedure Rules. Before either the prosecution or the defense may request disclosure under the rules, both parties must make a good faith attempt to resolve all discovery issues informally. Pennsylvania has **reciprocal discovery**, so that not only is the prosecution required to provide the defense with certain information, but the defense is also required to provide specified information to the prosecution.

Trial

The vast majority of all criminal cases are disposed of by a plea of guilty on the part of the defendant. If the defendant enters a plea of not guilty, the case will go to **trial**. According to the Sixth Amendment to the U.S. Constitution, all defendants have the right to a speedy and public trial by an impartial jury. These rights are also guaranteed by the Pennsylvania State Constitution.[52] However, the state Constitution also guarantees that in criminal cases the Commonwealth has the same right to a trial by jury as does the accused.[53] Therefore, a defendant may only waive his or her right to a **jury trial** if the attorney for the Commonwealth also waives the right of the Commonwealth to a trial by jury.[54] In these cases, the defendant will be given a **bench trial**. A bench trial is held before a judge and there is no jury present. A jury trial includes a total of twelve jurors, as well as one or more alternate jurors. If a juror must be excused during a trial (e.g., because of illness or family emergency), the alternate juror replaces the absent juror so that the trial may continue.

Jury Selection

The first step in a jury trial is the **selection of the jury**. The **venire**, or list of potential jurors, is compiled from voter registration rolls, drivers' license records, persons listed in the telephone directories, persons who pay taxes, and other similar lists.[55] Essentially, almost anyone who is a resident of the county in which the trial is being held, and who is of age to vote is eligible. Individuals who are ineligible for jury service in Pennsylvania include anyone who:

- cannot read, write, speak, and/or understand English

- is physically or mentally incapable of serving as a juror

- has been convicted of a crime that is punishable by imprisonment for over one year, and who has not been granted a pardon or amnesty

- is not a U.S. citizen and a citizen of the Commonwealth[56]

In addition, Pennsylvania exempts or excuses from jury duty anyone who

- is actively serving in the armed forces of the U.S. or the state

- has served on a jury for more than three days within the last three years or anyone who has served on a jury for less than three days within the last year

- can show the court that service would present undue hardship or extreme inconvenience

- is a spouse, child, sibling, parent, grandparent, or grandchild of a victim of criminal homicide[57]

The process of jury selection is known as **voir dire** and involves an examination of the prospective jurors by the court and by the attorneys for both the prosecution and the defense. The stated purpose of the *voir dire* is to determine whether each potential juror is impartial and will be able to render a fair verdict in a case. Potential jurors are placed under oath and then questioned by the judge, prosecutor, and defense attorney about their beliefs and backgrounds.

During the process of *voir dire*, both the defense and the district attorneys are allowed to make challenges, or to object to the inclusion of certain potential trial jurors. Pennsylvania allows two types of challenges. **Challenges for cause** generally are based on the attorney's belief that the juror is biased in some way that will prevent him or her from acting impartially and without prejudice during the trial. Both the defense attorney and the prosecutor have an unlimited number of challenges for good cause. **Peremptory challenges** may be used by either attorney to remove potential jurors from the jury panel without giving any specific reasons. The number of peremptory challenges allowed varies with the seriousness of the offense with which the defendant is charged. If the defendant has been charged with a misdemeanor, the Commonwealth and the defendant are each entitled to five peremptory challenges. If the trial involves a non-capital felony, seven peremptory challenges are allowed each side, and if the trial involves a capital felony, the prosecution and the defense are each entitled to twenty peremptory challenges. Additional peremptory challenges are allowed if there are multiple defendants and for the selection of alternate jurors.[58]

After the jury is selected, they are sworn in with the following oath:

> You do solemnly swear by Almighty God that you will well and truly try the issue joined between the Commonwealth and the defendant(s), and a true verdict render according to the evidence.[59]

Opening Statements

Both the prosecutor and the defense attorney are entitled to make an opening statement which provides all the participants in the trial, especially the jury, with an overview of the facts of the case. In Pennsylvania, the Commonwealth (the prosecution) presents its opening statement first. After the prosecution's opening remarks are completed, the defense may make an opening statement or may choose to wait until the start of the defense case.[60]

Presentation of the Prosecution's Evidence

After the opening statements are completed, the prosecution begins to present evidence in support of the charge that has been brought against the defendant. The prosecution presents first because the state is bringing the charge against the defendant and, because of the presumption of innocence, has assumed the burden of proof. Evidence submitted into court may include documents, pictures, recordings, depositions, objects, pictures, or witness testimony.

The prosecutor generally begins with **direct examination** of the prosecution's first witness, who is obviously expected to give evidence to support the state's case against the defendant. After the prosecutor finishes questioning the witness, the defense is allowed to **cross-examine** the same witness. If the prosecutor wishes, s/he may then return to ask the witness more questions in a process known as **re-direct examination**. Following this, the defense attorney has the option to question the witness once more during the **re-cross examination**. This procedure is repeated for each witness called by the prosecution.

Presentation of the Defense's Evidence

After the prosecution has presented all its evidence and called all its witnesses, the defense may then offer evidence. If the defense attorney chose not to make an opening statement at the start of the trial, s/he may make one now. The defense then proceeds to present its evidence. The procedure for the presentation of the evidence by the defense is similar to that of the prosecution: direct examination, cross examination, re-direct, and re-cross. The defendant is not required to testify at any point in the trial; both the U.S. Constitution and the Pennsylvania State Constitution protect the defendant against self-incrimination.[61]

Rebuttal and Surrebuttal

After the defense has presented its evidence, the prosecution is entitled to present a **rebuttal** case. At this time, the prosecutor may present evidence in response to the case presented by the defense. The defense may also be entitled to present a **surrebuttal** case, which involves presenting evidence in response to the rebuttal.

Closing Arguments

Once all the evidence is presented, each side is given the opportunity to make a **closing argument** which is addressed directly to the jury. Closing arguments are not used to present additional evidence. Each attorney reviews and summarizes the evidence that best supports his or her side of the case, discusses any inferences that may be drawn from that evidence, and points out weaknesses in the opponent's case. In Pennsylvania, the defense makes its closing arguments first, followed by the Commonwealth.[62]

Instructions to the Jury

After the closing arguments are completed, the judge provides **instructions to the jury** regarding any legal issues or points of law which are applicable to the case. This step is sometimes referred to as **charging the jury**.

Jury Deliberation and Verdict Rendition

After the judge has given instructions to the jury, the jury retires to the jury room for **deliberation**. At this time, the jurors discuss the case and attempt to come to agreement on a verdict concerning the guilt or innocence of the defendant. Pennsylvania law requires that all jurors agree unanimously on a guilty verdict before the defendant can be convicted of the charge.[63] If the jurors are unable to agree on a **verdict** after a reasonable period of time, they are **deadlocked** and considered to be a "**hung jury**." If this happens, the judge will declare a **mistrial** and the case may have to be retried in front of a new jury. If the jurors come to an agreement on a verdict, they are returned to the courtroom and the verdict is read in open court. After the verdict is read, but before it is recorded, either the defense or the Commonwealth may request that the jury be polled.[64] This is done to ensure that each member of the jury agrees with the verdict and that no member was coerced or intimidated into agreeing or agreed simply out of exhaustion.

If the verdict of the jury is not guilty, the trial is over and the defendant must be immediately discharged from custody and is entitled to the return of any bail money and the exoneration of any sureties. The trial court judge is required to accept a verdict of not guilty. Because of the state and federal constitutional protections against double jeopardy, the defendant may never be tried in state court on the same charges.

Proceedings Between the Verdict and the Sentence

If the defendant is found guilty (or has pled guilty or *nolo contendere*), s/he has the right to be sentenced without unreasonable delay. However, after a verdict of guilty is rendered and before the sentencing phase of the trial, the defendant may make a **post-trial motion** to set aside or modify the verdict. If the judge sets aside the verdict, the defendant may be entitled to a dismissal, a reduction of the charges, or a new trial. These motions are rarely granted. However, if a new trial is granted, the defendant may not be prosecuted for an offense that is more serious than that of which s/he was originally convicted. For example, if in the original trial the defendant was charged with second degree murder, s/he cannot be charged with first degree murder in the new trial.

The Sentence

If the defendant is found guilty, s/he will be sentenced by a judge. In most cases, the trial judge will pronounce the **sentence**, although in some situations it may be necessary for sentence to be pronounced by a different judge. The sentencing process is discussed in more detail in Chapter 6.

Appeal

If the defendant has been convicted of a crime, the court is required to notify the defendant of his or her right to **appeal** the judgment. The defendant has the right to appeal regardless of the crime of which s/he was convicted, the sentence received, or the type of trial.

An appeal does not involve retrying a case or even re-examining the factual issues surrounding the crime. It only involves an examination or review of the legal issues involved in the case. The purpose of an appeal is to make certain that the defendant received a fair trial and that s/he was not deprived of any constitutional rights at any time. In most cases, if a defendant wins on appeal, s/he will be re-tried.

NOTES

1. Pennsylvania's Unified Judicial System website
    (http://www.courts.state.pa.us/Index/UJS/Indexujs.asp)
2. 28 U.S.C. §118
3. 28 U.S.C. §41
4. Pennsylvania's Unified Judicial System website, *op cit.*
5. Pennsylvania State Constitution, Article 5, §12
6. Pennsylvania State Constitution, Article 5, §15
7. 42 Pa.C.S. §501
8. 42 Pa.C.S. §326(a)
9. Pennsylvania State Constitution, Article 5, §10(a)
10. 42 Pa.C.S. §721
11. 42 Pa.C.S. §722
12. 42 Pa.C.S. §723 and §724
13. 42 Pa.C.S. §726
14. The Superior Court of Pennsylvania website (http://www.superior.court.state.pa.us/)
15. *Ibid*
16. 42 Pa.C.S. §742
17. The Superior Court of Pennsylvania website, *op cit.*
18. 42 Pa.C.S. §761
19. 42 Pa.C.S. §762
20. 42 Pa.C.S. §901 and §911
21. Pennsylvania's Unified Judicial System website, *op cit.*
22. *Ibid*
23. 42 Pa.C.S. §951
24. The Philadelphia Courts website (http://courts.phila.gov/common-pleas/)
25. Pennsylvania's Unified Judicial System website, *op cit.*
26. Pennsylvania State Constitution, Article 5, §12
27. Pennsylvania's Unified Judicial System website, *op cit.*
28. Pittsburgh Municipal Courts website (http://www.city.pittsburgh.pa.us/mc/)
29. The Philadelphia Courts website, *op cit.*
30. Pennsylvania's Unified Judicial System website, *op cit.*
31. Administrative Office of Pennsylvania Courts website
    (http://www.courts.state.pa.us/Index/Aopc/IndexAOPC.asp)
32. Pennsylvania Bar Association website (http://www.pabar.org/)

33.   Pennsylvania Bar Institute website (http://www.pbi.org/)

34.   Pennsylvania's Unified Judicial System website, *op cit.*

35.   Pennsylvania Board of Law Examiners website (http://www.pabarexam.org/Default.htm)

36.   *Ibid*

37.   234 Rule 513 *et seq.*

38.   42 Pa.C.S.§8902(a)

39.   234 Rule 519(B)

40.   234 Rule 519(A)

41.   234 Rule 540(B)

42.   *Stack v. Boyle*, 342 U.S. 1 (1951)

43.   Pennsylvania State Constitution, Article 1, §14

44.   234 Rule 523

45.   234 Rule 543

46.   234 Rule 560

47.   234 Rule 562

48.   234 Rule 571

49.   234 Rule 590

50.   234 Rule 570

51.   234 Rule 578 *et seq.*

52.   Pennsylvania State Constitution, Article 1, §9

53.   Pennsylvania State Constitution, Article 1, §6

54.   234 Rule 620

55.   42 Pa.C.S. §4521

56.   42 Pa.C.S. §4502

57.   42 Pa.C.S. §4503

58.   234 Rule 634

59.   234 Rule 640

60.   234 Rule 604

61.   See the United States Constitution, Amendment V and the Pennsylvania State Constitution, Article 1, §9

62.   234 Rule 604

63.   234 Rule 648

64.   *Ibid*

CHAPTER 6

SENTENCING IN PENNSYLVANIA

INTRODUCTION

After a criminal defendant pleads guilty or is found guilty in court by a judge or jury, the judge must impose punishment upon the offender. A **sentence** is the penalty imposed by the court upon the defendant for the crime of which the defendant has been found guilty. In every case in which an offender has been convicted of an offense, the court is required to pronounce sentence. If the defendant has been found guilty on multiple counts, the court must pronounce sentence on each count.

The Pennsylvania Commission on Sentencing discusses the purpose of a sentence in 204 Pa.Code §303.11(a), stating that:

> In writing the sentencing guidelines, the Pennsylvania Commission on Sentencing strives to provide a benchmark for the judges of Pennsylvania. The sentencing guidelines provide sanctions proportionate to the severity of the crime and the severity of the offender's prior conviction record. This establishes a sentencing system with a primary focus on retribution, but one in which the recommendations allow for the fulfillment of other sentencing purposes including rehabilitation, deterrence, and incapacitation.

Thus, it appears clear that the primary purpose of sentencing in Pennsylvania is retribution, although other goals of sentencing may also be considered by the court in determining the final sentence.

TYPES OF SENTENCES

A variety of sentences may be imposed upon convicted offenders in Pennsylvania. Sentences acceptable in the Pennsylvania courts include:

- guilt without further penalty
- monetary fine
- mandatory restitution
- probation
- partial or total confinement (e.g., incarceration in a state or county facility)
- an intermediate sanction (e.g., work camp or electronic monitoring)
- death

81

Combinations of these sentences are allowed and may be imposed consecutively or concurrently. For example, a judge may order both imprisonment and a fine, or order an offender to pay both a fine and victim restitution.[1]

The court is expected to select a sentence based on three factors:

- the protection of society

- the seriousness of the offense based on its impact on both the victim and the community

- the rehabilitative needs of the defendant being sentenced

The court is also required to consider the requirements set forth in the sentencing guidelines adopted by the Pennsylvania Commission on Sentencing.[2]

WHEN SENTENCING OCCURS

After a defendant charged with a felony offense is found to be guilty (either by a guilty verdict at trial or by a plea of guilty or *nolo contendere*), s/he has a legal right to be sentenced without any unreasonable delay.[3] According to Rule 704 of the Pennsylvania Rules of Criminal Procedure, in most cases sentence must be imposed within 90 days after the defendant is found guilty. The sentence must be imposed by the same judge who presided at the trial, unless there are compelling reasons why s/he cannot be present.[4]

Prior to the imposition of a sentence, the judge may request several aids to sentencing including a psychiatric or psychological examination and/or a **presentence investigation report**. The presentence investigation is conducted by the county probation and parole department and provides the sentencing judge with relevant information on the background of the defendant. The report includes details about the circumstances of the crime; the defendant's prior record; family and employment history; mental, physical, and emotional health; education; financial information; military service, and any other information that may be of use to the judge. In addition, the report includes a victim impact statement.[5]

PENNSYLVANIA SENTENCING GUIDELINES

In 1982, an initial system of sentencing guidelines went into effect in Pennsylvania. However, in 1987 the guidelines were invalidated by the Pennsylvania Supreme Court due to a procedural error that occurred in 1981. A new set of guidelines were drafted and went into effect in 1988. These were revised and amended several times. The current sentencing guidelines became effective in June 1997. The sentencing guidelines "are designed to structure the discretion of the sentencing court without denying the court the power to craft sentences to the particular needs of the defendant and the interests of justice."[6] However, unlike the procedure in some states, in Pennsylvania judges are permitted to consider a variety of factors that are not included in the guidelines. In addition, the guidelines are not mandatory, although if a judge deviates from the guidelines, s/he is required to provide a written explanation of the reasons for the departure.

The Pennsylvania Commission on Sentencing

In 1978, the Pennsylvania General Assembly established the **Pennsylvania Commission on Sentencing**, with the goal of creating a "consistent and rational statewide sentencing policy that would increase sentencing severity for serious crimes and promote fairer and more uniform sentencing practices."[7] The Commission is made up of eleven members, including two members of the House of Representatives who are appointed by the Speaker of the House, two members of the state Senate who are appointed by the President pro tempore, four judges appointed by the Chief Justice of the Commonwealth, and three members appointed by the governor. These must include a district attorney, a defense attorney and a criminologist or professor of law. All members serve two-year terms.[8]

The Commission has a number of powers and duties, which are enumerated in 42 Pa.C.S. §2153. Their primary duty is to:

> develop sentencing guidelines which would
> 1) specify a range of sentences applicable for crimes of a given degree of gravity
> 2) specify a range of sentences of increased severity for defendants previously convicted of one or more felony or misdemeanor offenses, or convicted of a crime involving the use of a deadly weapon; and
> 3) prescribe variations from the range on account of aggravating or mitigating circumstances.[9]

Other responsibilities include establishing a research and development program to study issues such as guideline compliance, serving as an information clearinghouse, consulting with state courts as needed, collecting and disseminating information on sentence imposition and effectiveness, making recommendations regarding the modification or enactment of statutes related to sentencing or corrections to the General Assembly, and monitor judicial compliance with sentencing guidelines and mandatory sentencing laws.[10]

Factors Considered in Sentencing

The sentencing guideline model used in Pennsylvania considers two main factors: the seriousness of the offense and the prior record of the offender. The first factor to be considered is the **offense gravity score** (OGS). Each offense in the Crimes Code has been assigned a specific offense gravity score, ranging from a low of 1 to a high of 14.[11] If the crime involves ethnic intimidation, the OGS is increased by one point. The second factor is the **prior record score** (PRS). This is based on the type and number of prior adult convictions and juvenile adjudications. Each conviction is given a point value, ranging from a low of 1 to a high of 4, based on the conviction offense.[12] There are a total of eight PRS categories. The **Repeat Violent Offender Category** (REVOC) includes offenders with at least two prior convictions or adjudications for four-point offenses and whose current conviction has an OGS of 9 or higher. The **Repeat Felony 1/Felony 2 Offender Category** (RFEL) includes offenders with prior convictions or adjudications for Felony 1 or Felony 2 offenses that have a combined score of at least 6, but who do not meet the criteria for REVOC. The other categories are point-based, ranging from 0 to 5, for any offenders who do not fall into either REVOC or RFEL. The PRS category is determined by adding together the values of all prior convictions or adjudications, up to a maximum of five points.[13]

Using the Sentencing Guidelines Grid

The **basic sentencing matrix** contains most of the sentence recommendations. It merges the offense gravity score (on the grid columns) and the prior record score (on the grid rows) and provides the appropriate sentencing range in the intersecting cell.[14] The matrix is divided into five sentencing levels. **Level 1** calls for **restorative sanctions** for the least serious crimes and offenders. Restorative sanctions are those that do not involve confinement, such as probation, outpatient treatment programs, community service, and fines. Sanctions that may be imposed for an offender falling into **Level 2** include both confinement and non-confinement options. Sentencing options include restorative sanctions, **restrictive intermediate punishments**, or total or partial incarceration in a county facility for less than 12 months. Restrictive intermediate punishments include sanctions that strictly supervise the offender, such as work camps, halfway houses, work release centers, or house arrest with electronic monitoring or intensive supervision. The grid cell identifies the appropriate options and, in the case of incarceration, shows the minimum recommended number of months. **Level 3** provides recommendations for serious offenders and offenders with a large number of prior convictions. Options include incarceration in either a state or county facility, boot camp, or restrictive intermediate punishment. **Level 4** includes very serious offenders and those with a very large number of prior convictions. Sentences include boot camp or incarceration in a state facility for a minimum of 12 months. Finally, **Level 5**, the most serious level, generally includes the most serious and violent offenders and those with major drug convictions, and calls for incarceration in a state facility.[15] In addition, a fine or order of restitution may be added to any guideline sentence.[16]

In addition to the basic sentencing matrix, there are two Deadly Weapon Enhancement (DWE) sentencing matrices available to the court. The **DWE/Possessed Matrix** is used if the court has determined that the offender possessed a deadly weapon during the commission of the crime.[17] The **DWE/Used Matrix** is considered if the court has determined that the offender used a deadly weapon during the commission of the crime.[18] These matrices only include Levels 3, 4, and 5 and only specify sentences of incarceration.

The guidelines also provide for a **youth/school enhancement**, which increases the sentencing recommendations if the offender distributes a controlled substance to a minor or commits certain drug offenses within 1,000 feet of a school.[19]

Mandatory Sentences

For some crimes, the court is required by statute to impose a mandatory sentence. The statutory mandate overrides the sentencing guidelines. Most mandatory sentences in the statutes are mandatory minimum sentences; in most cases, the court may impose a longer sentence than that specified by statute. The most obvious exceptions are the penalties for first degree murder (death or life imprisonment) and second degree murder (life imprisonment).

Most mandatory sentencing provisions are determined by a specific characteristic of the crime, such as the type and the amount of drug involved in a drug-trafficking offense. The guidelines, in contrast, consider other factors such as the offender's prior record. As a result, in some cases, the sentence recommended by the guidelines may be longer than that mandated by the mandatory sentencing provision. In those situations, the court must consider the guidelines prior to imposing a sentence. If the court departs from the recommendations of the sentencing guidelines, a written explanation for the departure must be entered into the record.[20]

Departing from the Sentencing Guidelines

Although the sentencing grid provides a specific sentencing range, the judge does have the option of imposing a sentence outside this range. To do so, s/he must state, in writing, the reasons for the departure. Departures generally fall into three types or categories. **Dispositional departures** occur when the recommended sentence is a term of incarceration but the actual sentence imposed does not involve incarceration. **Durational departures** involve the imposition of a sentence that does not fall within the length recommended by the guidelines. Durational departures may fall above the guidelines (the court imposes a longer sentence than that recommended) or below the guidelines (the court imposes a shorter sentence). Finally, **procedural departures** occur when the court ignores a specific guideline procedure.[21]

VICTIM RIGHTS AND SERVICES

The Rights of Victims of Crime

In Pennsylvania, the term **victim** includes the following:

1. A direct victim.
2. A parent or legal guardian of a child who is a direct victim, except when the parent or legal guardian of the child is the alleged offender.

3. A family member of a homicide victim, including stepbrothers or stepsisters, stepchildren, stepparents or a fiance, one of whom is to be identified to receive communication as provided for in this act, except where the family member is the alleged offender.[22]

A **direct victim** is defined as:

An individual against whom a crime has been committed or attempted, and who, as a direct result of the criminal act or attempt, suffers physical or mental injury, death or the loss of earnings under this act. The term shall not include the alleged offender...[23]

18 P.S. §11-201 contains the **Pennsylvania Victim Bill of Rights**. This lists a number of basic rights and services to which all crime victims are entitled. The Bill of Rights applies to all crimes and victims and provides victims with the following rights:

1. To receive basic information concerning the services available for victims of crime.

2. To be notified of certain significant actions and proceedings within the criminal justice system pertaining to their case.

3. To be accompanied at all public criminal proceedings by a family member, a victim advocate or another person.

4. In cases involving personal injury crimes, burglary or violations of 75 Pa.C.S. §3731 (relating to driving under influence of alcohol or controlled substance) which involve bodily injury, to submit prior comment to the prosecutor's office on the potential reduction or dropping of any charge or changing of a plea.

5. To have opportunity to offer prior comment on the sentencing of a defendant, to include the submission of a written victim impact statement detailing the physical, psychological and economic effects of the crime on the victim and the victim's family and to have such comment considered by the judge when determining the defendant's sentence.

6. To be restored, to the extent possible, to the precrime economic status through the provision of restitution; compensation; and the expeditious return of property which is seized as evidence in the case when, in the judgment of the prosecutor, the evidence is no longer needed for prosecution of the case.

7. In personal injury crimes where the offender is sentenced to a State correctional facility, to be:
   i   given the opportunity to provide prior comment on and to receive State postsentencing release decisions, including work release, furlough, parole, pardon or community treatment center placement; and
   ii provided immediate notice of an escape of the offender.

8. In personal injury crimes where the offender is sentenced to a local correctional facility, to:

        i   receive notice of the date of the release of the offender, including work release, furlough, parole or community treatment center placement; and

       ii   be provided with immediate notice of an escape of the offender.

9. If the offender is subject to an order under 23 Pa.C.S. Ch. 61 (relating to protection from abuse) and is committed to a local correctional facility for a violation of the order or for a personal injury crime against a victim protected by the order, to receive immediate notice of the release of the offender on bail.

10. To receive notice if an offender is committed to a mental health facility from a State correctional institution and notice of the discharge, transfer or escape of the offender from the mental health facility.

11. To have assistance in the preparation of, submission of and follow-up on financial assistance claims to the bureau.

It is clear that a number of agencies within the criminal justice system have responsibilities toward the victim under the Bill of Rights. However, the victim also has responsibilities. For example, the victim must provide required information, such as a valid address and telephone number, to any agency that is responsible under the Bill of Rights to provide information and/or notice to the victim. If the information changes (e.g., if the victim moves), it is the victim's responsibility to update the agencies.[24]

Victim Impact Statements

A **victim impact statement** is a written or verbal statement that allows victims to provide input into the sentencing and parole decisions of offenders. Victim impact statements allow victims to explain to the decision-making body how the crime affected their lives, and the lives of their family and friends. A victim also has the option of choosing not to make a victim impact statement; it is a right, not a requirement.

The pre-sentencing investigation report, which is given to the judge for consideration when sentencing the defendant, includes written victim impact information.[25] The statement includes admissible evidence concerning the financial, psychological, and physical impact or effects of the crime upon the victim and his or her family.[26] If the direct victim has died from causes related to the crime, a family member may submit the victim impact statement. The prosecutor's office is required by law to notify the victim of the opportunity to submit a victim impact statement and to assist any victim to requests help in preparing the statement.[27]

In addition, victim impact information may be presented to the appropriate board or department when an offender is being considered for parole. These statements may be made either orally or in writing and shall be considered by the parole board when determining whether or not to grant release and what conditions of release should be imposed.[28]

The Right to Restitution

In Pennsylvania, **restitution** is defined as "the return of the property of the victim or payments in cash or the equivalent thereof pursuant to an order of the court."[29] In general, if an offender is convicted of a crime involving the theft, damage, or destruction of property, or any crime that caused personal injury to the victim, the offender shall be sentenced to make **restitution** in addition to any other punishment imposed by the judge.[30] If the offender has been ordered to make restitution and is placed on probation or parole, compliance with the order of restitution may be made a condition of release.[31]

The court may order the offender to make restitution in a lump sum payment or by monthly installments, or by some other payment schedule decided upon by the court. The offender may be ordered to make restitution to more than one person at the same time. In this situation, the court will prioritize payments, with the victim always being the highest priority. In general, the court is required to order restitution payments be made in the order of:

1. The crime victim
2. The Crime Victim's Compensation Board (to repay the Board for compensation paid to the victim)
3. Any other government agency that has reimbursed the victim for losses resulting from the crime
4. Any insurance company that has reimbursed the victim for losses resulting from the crime[32]

Individuals eligible for restitution include those who have suffered property damage or loss, monetary expenses, physical injury, or death as a result of the crime. If the victim is deceased, the victim's next of kin may be eligible for restitution. Expenses for which the offender may be required to make restitution include the cost of necessary medical, psychiatric, and psychological care; the cost of necessary physical or occupational therapy and rehabilitation; the cost of necessary funeral services; and reimbursement for income that was lost as a result of the offense.

The Right to Compensation

In addition to restitution, victims may be eligible for **compensation** through the **Victims Compensation Assistance Program** (V-CAP) of the **Pennsylvania Commission on Crime and Delinquency.** To be eligible for compensation, an individual must be the victim of a crime that occurred in Pennsylvania or a Pennsylvania resident who was injured or killed in a terrorist attack outside the United States. The victim must report the crime to the proper authorities within three days or file a Protection from Abuse Order within three days. Exceptions to the three-day limit may be made for good cause or if the victim is a minor. In addition, the victim must cooperate with law enforcement, the court system, and V-CAP. Finally, the application for compensation must be filed within two years of the date of the crime, although exceptions may be made if the victim is a minor.[33]

Not all crime-related expenses are covered by victims' compensation. Victim compensation benefits are available for the following expenses:

- necessary medical expenses, including physical therapy, home health care, and ambulance fees, as well as medication and supplies

- the cost of mental health counseling for direct victims, certain individuals who are in some way related to or living with the direct victim (including an individual engaged to or maintaining a common-law relationship with the direct victim), and individuals who witness a violent crime or discover a homicide victim

- funeral expenses for a deceased victim

- lost wages for a victim who missed work because of a physical or emotional disability related to the crime

- loss of support for financial dependants of a homicide victim who earned an income at the time of the crime

- stolen benefit cash (including Social Security, pension/retirement payments, or court-ordered child or spousal support) if this benefit is the victim's primary source of income and the cash was either stolen or taken by fraud

- relocation expenses for a direct victim and others living in the household when necessary for the immediate protection of their health and/or safety. The need to relocate must be verified by a law enforcement officer or a medical or human service provider

- crime scene cleanup of a personal living space, including the removal of blood or other stains resulting from the crime or any debris from the crime scene processing

Expenses that are not covered by victim's compensation include compensation for pain and suffering and the replacement of stolen or damaged property (with the exception of replacing necessary medical devices.)[34]

Compensation is intended to be the last resort for victims, so that only those costs which cannot and have not been reimbursed from some other source may be claimed for compensation. Therefore, if the victim has medical insurance which will cover the cost of medical care, or long-term disability insurance to cover loss of wages, the victim may not request victim compensation for these costs. Similarly, if the offender has been ordered to make restitution for some of the crime-related expenses, the victim may not apply for compensation to cover those expenses. In addition, only those expenses that are directly related to the crime may be eligible for compensation.

Obviously, the victim compensation program does not have an unlimited budget. Therefore, the state has placed limits on the amount of compensation that may be received by each victim. In most cases, the maximum total award of compensation is $35,000. Certain types of losses also have maximum award limits. For example, the maximum award for loss of earnings is $15,000 and the maximum award for loss of support is $20,000. However expenses for counseling, crime-scene cleanup, and forensic rape examination are not included in the $35,000 maximum award limit.[35]

NOTES

1.   42 Pa.C.S. §9721(a)
2.   42 Pa.C.S. §9721(b)
3.   42 Pa.C.S. §9752
4.   42 Pa.C.S. §9751
5.   Pennsylvania Rules of Criminal Procedure, Rule 702
6.   Pennsylvania Commission on Sentencing website (http://pcs.la.psu.edu/)
7.   *Ibid*
8.   42 Pa.C.S. §2152
9.   Pennsylvania Commission on Sentencing website, *op cit.*
10.   *Ibid*
11.   See 204 Pa.Code §303.15 for a listing of crimes and their associated offense gravity scores
12.   See 204 Pa.Code §303.7 for a listing of crimes and their associated points for the determination of the prior record score
13.   204 Pa.Code §303.1 *et seq.*
14.   204 Pa.Code §303.16
15.   204 Pa.Code §303.11
16.   204 Pa.Code §303.14
17.   204 Pa.Code §303.17
18.   204 Pa.Code §303.18
19.   204 Pa.Code §303.10
20.   Pennsylvania Commission on Sentencing website, *op cit.*
21.   *Ibid*
22.   18 P.S. §11-103
23.   *Ibid*
24.   18 P.S. §11-211
25.   Pennsylvania Rules of Criminal Procedure, Rule 702
26.   18 P.S. §11-201(5)
27.   18 P.S. §11-213(c)
28.   18 P.S. §11-214(c)
29.   18 Pa.C.S. §1106(h)

30.   18 Pa.C.S. §1106(a)
31.   18 Pa.C.S. §1106(b)
32.   18 Pa.C.S. §1106(c)
33.   Pennsylvania Commission on Crime and Delinquency website
         (http://www.pccd.state.pa.us/pccd/site/default.asp)
34.   *Ibid*
35.   *Ibid*

CHAPTER 7

CAPITAL PUNISHMENT IN PENNSYLVANIA

THE HISTORY OF CAPITAL PUNISHMENT IN PENNSYLVANIA

Pennsylvania has used death as the punishment for murder since the colonial days. During the colonial period, death was a mandatory punishment for a variety of crimes including murder, robbery, rape, burglary, and piracy. In 1794, however, in response to public arguments that the death penalty made it more difficult to obtain a conviction (because juries would fail to return a guilty verdict in cases where the death penalty was mandatory) and that it did not prevent crime, the Pennsylvania legislature abolished the death penalty as a punishment for all crimes other than first degree murder.

During and after the colonial period, the method used to carry out a sentence of death was public hanging. However, in 1834, Pennsylvania became the first state in the country to abolish public hangings and carry out executions in private. Until the early 20th century, each county was responsible for hanging offenders in private within the county jail.

In 1913, the method of execution was changed from hanging to electrocution and the responsibility for carrying out executions was transferred to the state. The first electric chair, known as "Old Smokey," was placed in the Western Penitentiary in Centre County (now the State Correctional Institution at Rockview). The first electrocution took place in 1915 and between 1915 and 1962, a total of 350 persons were electrocuted. Only two of these were women.[1]

No further executions occurred in Pennsylvania after 1962 because of concerns about the constitutionality of the death penalty. In 1972, the U.S. Supreme Court, in the case of *Furman v. Georgia*,[2] ruled that the death penalty, as it was administered, constituted "cruel and unusual punishment" and therefore was a violation of the Eighth Amendment of the U.S. Constitution. Later that year, based on the decision of the U.S. Supreme Court, the Pennsylvania Supreme Court ruled in the case of *Commonwealth v. Bradley*,[3] that the procedures used to sentence an offender to death in the Commonwealth were unconstitutional. At the time of the *Bradley* decision, approximately 24 offenders under sentences of death were in the Pennsylvania prison system awaiting execution. They were all released from death row and their sentences were commuted to life imprisonment.[4]

In 1974, the state legislature revised the death penalty law over the veto of Governor Milton Shapp. However, in 1977, the state Supreme Court overturned the new law in the case of *Commonwealth v. Moody*,[5] again declaring the death penalty as it was administered to be unconstitutional. The previous year, on January 15, 1976, the U.S. Supreme Court ruled in the case of *Gregg v. Georgia*[6] that capital punishment did not invariably violate the Constitution and reinstated the death penalty. In response to *Gregg* and *Moody*, the state legislature again redrafted the death penalty legislation. The new law was enacted in 1978, again over the veto of Governor Shapp. This law is still in effect and has withstood a number of appeals to the U.S. Supreme Court.[7]

In 1990, Governor Robert P. Casey approved legislation that changed the method used to carry out the sentence of death to **lethal injection**. The first execution by lethal injection was carried out on May 2, 1995. The Pennsylvania electric chair is currently the property of the Pennsylvania Historical and Museum Commission.[8]

CAPITAL PUNISHMENT IN PENNSYLVANIA TODAY

The only **capital crime** in Pennsylvania is the crime of first degree murder with aggravating circumstances. The method of execution currently used in Pennsylvania is lethal injection. There is no statutory minimum age to receive the death penalty in Pennsylvania. However, according to the 1988 U.S. Supreme Court ruling in *Thompson v. Oklahoma*,[9] the minimum permissible age to put an individual to death in the U.S. is 16, which is the limit used in Pennsylvania. Pennsylvania does not forbid the execution of a mentally retarded individual.[10]

Although the death penalty was reenacted after *Furman*, there were no executions in Pennsylvania until 1995. Between 1995 and 2004, there were a total of three executions in Pennsylvania. As of October 1, 2004, there were 224 inmates on death row in Pennsylvania. Of these, all but 5 are male. A racial breakdown shows that 61 percent are black, 31 percent are white, 7 percent are Hispanic, and 1 percent are Asian. Most of the male offenders awaiting death are housed at State Correctional Institution (SCI) Greene but some are held at SCI Graterford. Female offenders on death row are housed at SCI Muncy.[11]

SENTENCING IN CAPITAL CRIMES

Like many states that have capital punishment, Pennsylvania uses a bifurcated system with a the determination of guilt or innocence separated from the determination of the sentence. The sentencing hearing generally is held before the same jury that determined the defendant's guilt or innocence. If the defendant waived his or her right to a jury trial, or pleaded guilty to the crime, the sentencing hearing is held before a jury impaneled for the procedure. The defendant has the option of waiving the jury (if the Commonwealth consents); in this situation, the sentencing hearing is held before the trial judge.[12]

The purpose of the hearing is to determine the existence of aggravating and mitigating circumstances. There are 18 aggravating circumstances which may be considered by the jury or the court when determining the sentence in a case of first degree murder. For an offender to be sentenced to death, at least one of these aggravating circumstances must exist beyond a reasonable doubt. They fall into three main categories. Seven are victim based:

1. The victim was a police officer, firefighter, correctional officer, or worked at of the occupations listed in the statute and was killed while engaging in the performance of his or her duties or as a result of his or her official position.

2. The victim was held by the defendant, either for ransom or reward, or for use as a hostage or shield.

3. The victim was a prosecution witness killed to prevent him or her from testifying against the defendant.

4. The victim was involved, associated with, or competed with the defendant in the sale, manufacture, distribution, or delivery of a controlled substance and the victim's death was related to that association.

5. The victim was an informant and was killed in retaliation for his or her activities.

6. The victim was under the age of 12.

7. The victim was in her third trimester of pregnancy or the defendant knew she was pregnant.

Four of the circumstances focus on the defendant's prior criminal record:

1. The defendant has a significant history of convictions for violent felony offenses.

2. The defendant has a prior conviction or a crime for which a sentence of death or life imprisonment was a possible punishment, or was under sentence of life imprisonment at the time of the crime.

3. The defendant has a prior conviction for murder in any jurisdiction.

4. The defendant has prior conviction for voluntary manslaughter or a substantially equivalent crime in any other jurisdiction.

The final seven circumstances focus on circumstances surrounding the crime:

1. The defendant committed murder for hire.

2. The death of the victim occurred during an aircraft hijacking.

3. The defendant killed the victim during the commission of a felony.

4. While committing the crime, the defendant knowingly created a grave risk of death to someone other than the victim.

5. The crime was committed using torture.

6. The crime occurred during the perpetration of a felony under the Controlled Substance, Drug, Device and Cosmetic Act.

7. At the time of the crime, the defendant was under court order restricting his or her behavior toward the victim (e.g., a restraining order).[13]

There are also eight mitigating circumstances to be considered by the sentencing jury or court. Most relate to characteristics of the defendant but one of the seven is victim-based:

1. The victim participated in, or consented to, the act which led to his or her death.

Four of the mitigating circumstances are similar to defenses that the defendant might raise at trial. However, these factors, while acting to mitigate the offender's actions, are not sufficient to serve as a defense to the crime itself:

1. The defendant committed the crime under substantial duress or domination, although not substantial enough to be considered a complete defense to the crime (similar to the defense of duress).

2. The defendant's capacity to appreciate the criminality of his or her conduct, or to conform that conduct to the requirements of the law was substantially impaired (similar to the defense of insanity).

3. The defendant was under the influence of an extreme mental or emotional disturbance (also related to the insanity defense).

4. The age of the defendant at the time of the crime (similar to the defense of age negating criminal responsibility, even though the offender is old enough to be criminal responsible).

The final three circumstances focus on the defendant's prior record and possible future danger s/he may pose:

1. The defendant has no significant prior criminal history.

2. The defendant's participation in the crime was relatively minor.

3. Any other evidence of mitigation as relating to the record and/or character of the defendant and the circumstances of the crime.[14]

During the sentencing hearing, evidence is presented to the judge and the jury. Evidence that is admissible at the sentencing hearing includes:

- evidence about the victim and the impact of the victim's death on the victim's family

- evidence about matters relating to aggravating or mitigating circumstances

- any other evidence the court considers admissible and relevant to the question of the sentence to be imposed[15]

The jury (or the judge if the sentencing hearing is held before the court) must first determine whether or not at least one of the aggravating factors exists. If the jury does not find the presence of one or more aggravating factors beyond a reasonable doubt, the defendant may not be sentenced to death but will receive a sentence of imprisonment for life. If the jury finds the presence of at least one aggravating factor beyond a reasonable doubt, it must then determine whether any mitigating factors exist, based on a preponderance of the evidence (note that the burden of proof for mitigating circumstances is lower than for aggravating circumstances). If there are no mitigating circumstances, the verdict must be a sentence of death. If the jury finds that at least one mitigating circumstance exists, it must then determine, whether the mitigating circumstances are outweighed by the aggravating circumstances. If the jury finds that the aggravating circumstances outweigh the mitigating circumstances, the offender will be sentenced to death. If the jury finds that the mitigating circumstances outweigh the aggravating circumstances, the defendant will be sentenced to life imprisonment.[16]

Every capital case in Pennsylvania is subject to automatic review by the Supreme Court of Pennsylvania. The Court does not have the discretion to reject appeals in capital cases. No defendant may be executed until his or her conviction and sentence have been reviewed by the Court.[17]

THE LETHAL INJECTION PROCESS IN PENNSYLVANIA

Only two offenders have been put to death in Pennsylvania since the method of death was changed to lethal injection. Executions take place at SCI Rockview, in a separate maximum-security building located on the grounds of the prison. The complex includes three cells, which are intended to house condemned inmates for a short time prior to the actual execution.[18]

The state has three executioners who receive $300 each for carrying out an execution. They also receive an annual retainer and are paid to participate in mock "drills." According to the state, the execution team members are not employees of the state prison system and their identities are kept secret. Even their prison credentials have false names so that the staff members who participate in the training drills do not know their true names.[19]

Prior to the actual execution, the inmate may receive visitors, including immediate members of the family who have been approved by the Department of Corrections, a clergyman, and the inmate's attorney. The offender will be given an opportunity to make a final statement before the execution. Executions are witnessed by a clergyman, six news reporters, and six adult citizens selected by the warden of the prison.[20]

The state does not identify the exact drugs used in the lethal injection procedure but there are three drugs used: a barbiturate to put the inmate to sleep, a paralytic agent that paralyzes the skeletal muscles and stops breathing, and a drug that causes cardiac arrest and stops the heart from beating. The procedure takes approximately six to seven minutes.[21]

NOTES

1.   Pennsylvania Department of Corrections website (http://www.cor.state.pa.us/)
2.   *Furman v. Georgia*, 408 U.S. 238 (1972)
3.   *Commonwealth v. Bradley*, 295 A.2d 842 (Pa. 1972)
4.   Pennsylvania Department of Corrections website, *op cit.*
5.   *Commonwealth v. Moody*, 382 A.2d 442 (Pa. 1977), cert. den. 438 U. S. 914 (1978)
6.   *Gregg v. Georgia*, 428 U.S. 153 (1976)
7.   Pennsylvania Department of Corrections website, *op cit.*
8.   Ibid
9.   *Thompson v. Oklahoma*, 487 U.S. 815 (1988)
10.   Death Penalty Information Center website (http://www.deathpenaltyinfo.org/)
11.   Pennsylvania Department of Corrections website, *op cit.*
12.   42 Pa.C.S. §9711
13.   *Ibid*
14.   *Ibid*
15.   *Ibid*
16.   *Ibid*
17.   *Ibid*
18.   Pennsylvania Department of Corrections website, *op cit.*
19.   Roddy, D.B. (1995, April 23). "Secrecy governs execution process." *Pittsburgh Post-Gazette*, Two-Star Edition, p.A-14.
20.   *Ibid*
21.   *Ibid*

CHAPTER 8

CORRECTIONS IN PENNSYLVANIA

THE HISTORY OF PRISONS IN PENNSYLVANIA

The penal system in Pennsylvania began in 1682 when William Penn first suggested replacing punishments of torture and mutilation with hard labor in a house of correction. In 1773, Philadelphia's **Walnut Street Jail** was built. As the use of incarceration as a punishment increased, the **Philadelphia Society for Assisting Distressed Prisoners** was created in 1776 to investigate the conditions in local jails. The Society was renamed the **Philadelphia Society for Alleviating the Miseries of Public Prisons** in 1778 and is known today as the **Pennsylvania Prison Society.** The Society focused on the poor conditions in the Walnut Street Jail, criticizing the lack of segregation of prisoners (who were all housed together, regardless of age, gender, or seriousness of offense) proposing that more private, or even solitary, punishment would be a better way to reform offenders.

In 1790, in response to the Society's work, the **Walnut Street Jail** in Philadelphia was converted to solitary confinement, with 36 single cells built in the yard where prisoners had congregated together. However, the jail was soon overcrowded, defeating the intention of isolation. However, in 1821, the state authorized the construction of the **Eastern State Penitentiary** at Cherry Hill and the facility was opened in 1829. Pennsylvania had actually opened the **Western Penitentiary** at Pittsburgh three years earlier. However, because of the extremely small size of the cells and the lack of air and light, the facility quickly failed. As a result, Eastern State Penitentiary is considered the first modern prison in the United States.

Eastern State operated on the **Pennsylvania system** (also known as the **solitary system** or **separate system**). The emphasis was on total and uninterrupted solitary confinement; inmates worked, ate, and slept in individual solitary cells for the duration of their sentence. They were confined to their cells for 23 hours per day, with one hour per day of solitary exercise in a yard attached to the cell. The only visitors allowed were jailers and members of the clergy. Visits from family and friends were not allowed because they were part of the corrupting society that led the inmates into crime. The penitentiary was constructed to allow no communication between cells. While in their cells, prisoners were expected to work at various crafts and produce furniture, clothing, and other products for sale by the prison. Each cell contained a Bible and other religious literature but no other reading material. This was supposed to make the prisoner think about reformation and focus on personal spiritual development. While solitary confinement in the prison was a punishment, it was also a way to emphasize repentance. Isolation forced each prisoner to reflect on the error of his or her ways; thus the origin of the of the term "penitentiary," from the concept of penitence.

The separate system eventually was abandoned in Pennsylvania, partly because the total silence and isolation drove some of the inmates insane while others became ill or even committed suicide. In addition, the separate system was extremely expensive to run. By the Civil War, most states, including Pennsylvania, had abandoned the separate system. The Eastern State Penitentiary continued to operate until 1970. It is now a National Historic Landmark site open to the public.

PENNSYLVANIA DEPARTMENT OF CORRECTIONS

In 1953, after riots broke out in two Pennsylvania state prisons, the legislature created the **Devers Committee** to study the problem of prison unrest and to examine other prison problems. The committee, chaired by retired Major General Jacob L. Devers, focused on recommending ways to improve the Pennsylvania prison system. The Committee suggested that an agency be created to supervise, control, and administer the state prison system. In response to this, the legislature created the **Bureau of Corrections** in 1953.

The Bureau of Corrections administered the prison system in Pennsylvania until 1980, when constitutional changes disbanded the Justice Department in Pennsylvania. The Bureau was placed under the jurisdiction of the new Office of General Counsel to the Governor and in 1984 was made a cabinet-level agency and renamed the **Department of Corrections** (DOC). The mission of the DOC is to:

> protect the public by confining persons committed to our custody in safe, secure facilities, and to provide opportunities for inmates to acquire the skills and values necessary to become productive law-abiding citizens; while respecting the rights of crime victims.[1]

The DOC is responsible for 27 state correctional institutions (SCI), 14 community corrections centers, over 45 private community corrections facilities, and 1 boot camp. Almost all the facilities are accredited. The newest facility, SCI Forest was dedicated on September 29, 2004 and will house approximately 2,200 adult male offenders.[2]

PRISONS IN PENNSYLVANIA

As of December 31, 2003, the DOC population included 40,817 inmates. Of these, 95.6 percent were male and 4.6 percent were female. Of the male offenders, approximately 50 percent were white, 39 percent black, and 10 percent Hispanic. The mean age of the male offenders was 35. Of the female offenders, approximately 35 percent were white, 53 percent black, and 11 percent Hispanic. The mean age of female offenders was 36.[3]

In 2002, slightly over half (51 percent) of all inmates incarcerated in the Pennsylvania prison system were convicted of Part I offenses, including both violent and property crimes. Approximately 31 percent were convicted of Part II offenses, while the remainder (18 percent) were incarcerated for parole violations. Approximately 21 percent (8,440) of the inmates were serving long-term sentences (over 10 years). Of these, 3,859 were serving life sentences and 243 were on death row.[4]

There are five levels of custody or security in Pennsylvania correctional institutions, although some facilities may have multiple levels of security within the same institution. **Level 5** is the maximum security level and is reserved for inmates requiring direct and constant supervision. **Level 4** is known as close security, and is reserved for inmates who are still considered a security risk but who pose less of a threat than do Level 5 inmates. An inmate who is classified **Level 3** is considered medium security and **Level 2** inmates are considered to be eligible for incarceration in a minimum security facility. **Level 1** is reserved for inmates placed in Community Corrections Centers. An inmate's custody level will be reviewed annually and the inmate may be reclassified to a lower security level if s/he has shown proper behavior and active program participation.

As of December 31, 2003, the majority of inmates (78.5 percent) were classified as custody levels 2 (43 percent) or 3 (35.5 percent). Only approximately 3 percent of inmates have been classified as Level 1, 16 percent as Level 4, and 2 percent as Level 5.[5]

Approximately 4.4 percent of the state's prison population is female. DOC operates two facilities that house female offenders: SCI Muncy and SCI Cambridge Springs. Muncy houses all women offenders under sentence of death. Women offenders are less likely than men to be incarcerated for violent offenses (51 percent versus 66 percent) and are less likely to be serving a maximum sentence of at least 10 years (29 percent versus 45 percent).[6]

PRISON LABOR AND EDUCATION PROGRAMS

A variety of educational, vocational, and work programs are available for inmates in DOC facilities. However, not all programs are available in every institution.

Prison Labor in Pennsylvania

Prison labor was used in Pennsylvania since the colonial period. Inmates housed in the Walnut Street Jail performed public labor, cleaning and repairing city streets, as a form of punishment and discipline. However, after the Pennsylvania Prison Society denounced the public display of inmates at work, the use of public labor was eliminated. Inmates in the Walnut Street Jail who were sentenced to imprisonment at hard labor worked separately within the jail at activities such as weaving, shoemaking, nail making, and picking and carding wool and hair.

In the Western State Penitentiary, inmates were unable to work in solitary confinement due to the small size of the cells. They worked in congregate workshops, producing brooms, shoes, hosiery, and other products. Inmates in the Eastern State Penitentiary did work in their cells, doing handicrafts as a form of self-discipline and as a way of creating positive work habits. The primary industries were weaving and shoemaking; other inmates dyed cloth or picked oakum in their cells.

After the Civil War, the development of mechanical weaving machines made it virtually impossible for inmates working by hand to compete. In 1883, the state abolished the **contract system** of convict labor, which allowed outside contractors to employ inmates within the prison and to sell the products of their labor. It was replaced by the **public account system**, under which inmate labor was directed by the state and the items manufactured were sold by the state. New institutions such as the State Institutional Reformatory at Huntingdon were constructed with workshops, farms, and other facilities for inmate labor.

In 1897, the **Muehlbronner Act** was passed as a result of lobbying by labor organizations. The Act limited the type of labor prisoners could do, primarily prohibiting the use of power machinery in prisons, and limited the number of inmates that may be employed in any custodial institution to 35 percent. The Act practically eliminated prison industry in state penitentiaries by forcing inmates to produce products manually. In response to concerns about the Act by prison administrators, a prison labor commission was formed in 1913 to study the feasibility and advisability of allowing all inmates to be employed in prison labor. A second commission was appointed in 1915 to determine the types and location of prison industries. The 1915 Act also reversed the Muehlbronner Act's limitation on the percentage of inmates that could be employed and introduced the **state-use system**, which stated that all goods produced by inmates could be sold only to state institutions. Under this system, inmate-produced goods could not be sold on the open market. However, the Act did not require state institutions to purchase these products. In 1921, the General Assembly passed an Act creating the **Department of Public Welfare** and giving this Department control over prisons, as well as other institutions such as insane asylums. The Act also required that all institutions under the control of the Department purchase prison-made products and lifted the Muehlbronner Act's restriction on the use of power machinery in prisons. Since this time, prison industries have been essentially self-supporting.

In 1929, the Department of Public Welfare was given the authority to create an inmate work program, which eventually developed into the modern **Pennsylvania Correctional Industries (PCI)**. In 1953, the Devers Committee recommended that more prison industries be developed, as a way of reducing prison unrest. After the creation of the Bureau of Corrections, the number of correctional industries increased greatly, as did the percentage of inmates employed in prisons. However, in the 1980s the prison population began to increase dramatically, making it more difficult to place inmates in appropriate institutional and work environments. The prison industry system was unable to grow rapidly enough to meet the needs of the increasingly large inmate population. However, in the 1990s, the DOC focused its attention on the prison industry system, which was revised and improved and given a new focus on teaching inmates to work, rather than simply providing them with an opportunity to work.

Pennsylvania Correctional Industries

Pennsylvania Correctional Industries (PCI) is a division of the DOC that provides work opportunities to incarcerated offenders. As of April 2004, PCI employed over 1,600 inmates in 115 different jobs within the state prison system. To qualify for employment in PCI, an inmate must be free of misconduct and must have at least an 8ᵗʰ grade reading level. Eligibility is also dependent upon the inmate's treatment level, custody level, and length of sentence remaining. The pay scale ranges from 19¢ to 42¢ per hour, with production bonuses of up to 70¢ per hour. Up to 30 percent of inmate wages are returned to the counties for victim restitution, court costs, fines, and child support payments.[7]

Prison industries in Pennsylvania still operate under the state-use system, so goods and services produced by inmates may only be purchased by federal, state, and local governments, any state, educational, or charitable institution receiving state government aid, or any institution receiving aid from the federal government.[8]

Among the products produced by PCI inmate employees are:

- clothing (aprons, uniforms, belts, boots, caps, shirts, jeans, lab coats, t-shirts, sweat suits, undergarments, etc.)
- bed, bath, and personal care items (mattresses and mattress covers, pillows and pillow cases, sheets, towels, shower curtains, etc.)
- various types of container bags (book bags, attaches, garment bags, cartons, etc.)
- food products (beef, pork, fish, canned fruit and vegetables, fresh fruit, etc.)
- a wide variety of furniture (bookcases, dressers, desks, beds, nightstands, tables, shelves, stools, mirrors, etc.)
- cleaning and housekeeping items (brooms, brushes, cleaning compounds, soaps, etc.)
- recreation products and storage items (park benches, picnic tables, storage sheds, trash containers, etc.)

PCI also offers a wide range of services. including:

- laundry
- metal fabrication
- engraving and printing
- furniture refinishing and reupholstering
- optical
- shoe repair
- duplication

These products and services are produced at 34 shops in 19 state prisons.[9]

In addition to providing inmates with an opportunity to be employed and earn money while in prison, PCI provides inmates with the opportunity to learn job skills that will be of use after they are released from DOC custody. Inmates are required to comply with a work ethic, including punctuality, reliability, and dependability.

Inmate Educational Programs

The DOC's **Bureau of Correction Education** provides both academic and vocation education to help inmates develop skills necessary to obtain jobs upon release. All inmates who have a reading level of less than the 8th grade level are required to participate in Adult Basic Education (ABE) programming, which includes reading and math instruction, English as a Second Language, and peer tutoring. Special education programs are provided for qualifying inmates with documented learning or developmental disabilities. A Secondary Education program, focusing on GED preparation provides instruction for inmates who have not graduated from high school but who are too advanced (or who have completed) ABE instruction. All SCIs are licensed GED testing centers.

A small amount of educational programming is available for inmates who have graduated from high school or who have passed the GED. Inmates are charged $50 per course and may participate in various programs in vocational/business education offered by institutions of higher education. The Bureau also offers vocational education programs, which may lead to trade-based certificates or registration in an apprenticeship program.[10]

The Community Work Program

The DOC's Community Work Program allows inmates to participate in work projects to benefit local communities, nonprofit organizations, and state agencies. Projects in which inmate work crews have participated include highway cleanup, park restoration, and mural painting. Since 1995, the program has saved over $12 million for federal, state, local, and nonprofit agencies.[11]

Participation in any project that involves work outside the prison is limited to non-violent, minimum security offenders. However the program also provides opportunities for violent offenders, or those in maximum security facilities, to participate in in-house projects. For example, offenders serving life sentences at SCI Graterford participate in the "Wheels for the World" project, restoring used wheelchairs to be sent to other countries, such as China, Honduras, Romania, and Poland.[12]

COUNTY JAILS AND PRISONS IN PENNSYLVANIA

While state prisons in Pennsylvania are run by the DOC, **county prisons and jails** are operated at the county level. In many states, county facilities are run by the county sheriff's office. However, as discussed in Chapter 4, county sheriffs in Pennsylvania generally focus on law enforcement and court-related duties and not on the care and custody of inmates.

In general, county facilities house pretrial detainees and convicted offenders sentenced to a shorter term of incarceration. The maximum sentence allowed in a county prison may vary by county.

In general, county facilities tend to provide fewer programs and services than prisons because the population is much more transient and the length of stay is significantly shorter.

The Philadelphia Prison System

The **Philadelphia Prison System** (PPS) operates five facilities in Philadelphia County. The system is responsible for the custody of individuals awaiting trial and inmates serving sentences of up to two years. Approximately 61 percent of inmates housed in PPS are pre-trial detainees while the rest are convicted offenders. In addition, offenders from other counties may be held by the PPS while attending court proceedings in the county. The PPS provides inmates with a variety of educational, religious, self-help, vocational, and industrial training programs.

The **Curran-Fromhold Correctional Facility** (CFCF) opened in 1995 and is made up four housing buildings, each with eight housing units, known as pods. Each pot has 32 cells organized around a common living/dining area. In addition, the facility has an administration building. CFCF also functions as the intake center for all adult male inmates and detainees, processing almost 30,000 individuals each year. The facility's average census in Fiscal Year 2002 was 2,484 residents. The **Detention Center** primarily houses minimum-security adult males and had an average census of 1,362 in FY 2002. It also houses a prison health services wing with 99 beds for inmates who require inpatient medical or behavioral health treatment. The first **House of Correction** was built in 1874 but was dismantled in 1925 and a new facility was constructed on the original site using the original materials. It was opened in 1927 and had an average census in FY 2002 of 1,278. It was constructed on the radial design first used in the Eastern State Penitentiary and has 663 cells, most of which house two inmates. The majority of residents are adult males, although a small number of juveniles may be housed in segregated areas until reaching the age of 18. The **Philadelphia Industrial Correctional Center** had an average census of 1,175 in FY 2002. Until the completion of the **Women's Detention Facility**, female offenders were housed in the Center, which was divided into a female division with 250 cells, and a male division with 400 cells.[13]

The Allegheny County Jail

The first **Allegheny County Jail** was opened in 1884 and today is an historical landmark in the county. In the 1980s, the jail was placed under a federal court order requiring the county to deal with issues such as overcrowding and space limitations. In 1990, because the jail had not met constitutional standards, the county was ordered not to accept any more prisoners at the facility and to develop and plans for the construction of a new facility. A new jail was constructed in Pittsburgh and opened in 1995. The old jail facility is no longer used as a custodial facility but houses the family and juvenile sections of the Common Pleas Court.[14]

The new jail currently houses over 2,000 individuals, both male and female. The majority of the prisoners in the jail are pre-trial detainees. In 1999, a total of 22,858 inmates were received by the jail. The average number of days served per inmate was 29.71 and the total daily per capita cost per inmate was $62.27. Approximately 97 percent of the inmates received were held for court while the remaining 3 percent were sentenced by minor judiciary.[15]

COMMUNITY SUPERVISION PROGRAMS IN PENNSYLVANIA

Probation

Probation is a community-based sentence handed down by a court that involves contacts with probation officers and various other terms and conditions prescribed by law or assigned by the sentencing judge. If the offender violates any of these conditions, the court has the option to revoke probation and impose a sentence of incarceration. Probation in the United States was originally created in Boston in 1841 and became an official element of the state court system in 1878. In Pennsylvania, offenders on probation are supervised at the county level.

Offenders placed on probation generally are required to comply with a variety of conditions determined by the court. These may include any of the following:

- meeting any family responsibilities
- remaining employed or in school
- participating in a community service program
- participating in a medical or psychiatric treatment program, or in a drug or alcohol treatment program
- refraining from possessing a firearm or other dangerous weapon without written permission
- living within the jurisdiction of the sentencing court
- notifying the court or probation officer of any change of address or employment
- reporting to a probation officer or allowing the probation officer to visit the offender's home
- pay any imposed fines and/or victim restitution[16]

Some are general conditions, which are mandated for all offenders. Others are special conditions, which may be required of some but not all offenders. The sentencing court decides which of these, if any, will be mandated for the offender. If the offender complies with all the terms and conditions of probation and successfully completes the period of supervision assigned by the court, s/he will be released. Offenders who violate any of these conditions may have their probation revoked and be committed to state prison or county facility.

Parole

Unlike probation, **parole** is not a sentence. It is a conditional release from a sentence of incarceration in which offenders serve the remaining portion of their sentence in the community while participating in post-release community supervision. An offender is not eligible for parole until s/he has served the minimum sentence imposed by the court. The conditions for parole and probation are the same, and the state does not distinguish between the terms **probation officer** and **parole officer**.

If the offender's maximum sentence is less than two years, the parole decision is made by the sentencing judge and the offender is supervised at the county level. If the offender's maximum possible sentence is two years or more (even if the offender is serving his or her sentence in the county jail), the parole decision is made by the state **Board of Probation and Parole** (BPP), who also supervises the offender. The BPP is also responsible for specifying and modifying conditions of release and for returning parolees to custody if necessary.[17]

NOTES

1. Pennsylvania Department of Corrections web site (http://www.cor.state.pa.us/)
2. *Ibid*
3. Pennsylvania Department of Corrections (2004, April). *Female Offenders*. Available online at: http://www.cor.state.pa.us/stats/lib/stats/female.pdf
4. Pennsylvania Department of Corrections (2003, November). *Annual Statistical Report, 2002*. Available online at: http://www.cor.state.pa.us/stats/lib/stats/2002AnnualReport.pdf
5. Pennsylvania Department of Corrections (2004, April). *Diagnostic and Classification Procedure*. Available online at: http://www.cor.state.pa.us/stats/lib/stats/dc.pdf
6. Pennsylvania Department of Corrections (2004, April). *Female Offenders, op cit.*
7. Pennsylvania Department of Corrections (2004, April). *Pennsylvania Correctional Industries*. Available online at: http://www.cor.state.pa.us/stats/lib/stats/ci.pdf
8. Pennsylvania Correctional Industries web site (http://www.pci.state.pa.us/pci/site/default.asp)
9. Pennsylvania Department of Corrections (2004, April). *Pennsylvania Correctional Industries, op cit.*
10. Pennsylvania Department of Corrections (2004, September). *Correction Education*. Available online at: http://www.cor.state.pa.us/stats/lib/stats/edu.pdf
11. Pennsylvania Department of Corrections (2003, February). *Work Training Programs*. Available online at: http://www.cor.state.pa.us/stats/lib/stats/other%20work.pdf
12. Anonymous (2004, March). "Graterford involved in mural cleanup". *Graterfriends*, vol 24, #3, p 5.
13. Philadelphia Prison System web site (http://www.phila.gov/prisons/index.html)
14. Allegheny County Jail web site (http://www.county.allegheny.pa.us/jail/index.asp)
15. Allegheny County Jail (2000). *1999 Annual Report*. Available online at: http://www.county.allegheny.pa.us/jail/report.asp
16. 42 Pa.C.S. 9754
17. Pennsylvania Board of Probation and Parole web site (http://www.pbpp.state.pa.us/pbppinfo/site/default.asp)

CHAPTER 9

THE JUVENILE JUSTICE SYSTEM IN PENNSYLVANIA

JUVENILES AND THE LAW

The Pennsylvania Juvenile Act is found in Chapter 63 of Title 42 of the Pennsylvania Consolidated Statutes. The Act defines a **child** as:

> An individual who:
> (1) is under the age of 18 years;
> (2) is under the age of 21 years who committed an act of delinquency before reaching the age of 18 years; or
> (3) was adjudicated dependent before reaching the age of 18 years and who, while engaged in a course of instruction or treatment, requests the court to retain jurisdiction until the course has been completed, but in no event shall a child remain in a course of instruction or treatment pas the age of 21 years.[1]

A **delinquent child** is "a child ten years of age or older whom the court has found to have committed a delinquent act and is in need of treatment, supervision or rehabilitation."[2] A **delinquent act** is any act that would be considered a crime if it were committed by an adult.[3]

Essentially, under the Juvenile Act, a child under the age of ten is not considered to be responsible for his or her acts, and a person 18 years of age or older is considered to be an adult under the law. However, there are some exceptions to this. If a juvenile who is at least 15 years of age commits murder, s/he will automatically be charged as an adult. In addition, if a juvenile 15 years of age or older commits rape, involuntary deviate sexual intercourse, aggravated assault, robbery, robbery of a motor vehicle, aggravated indecent assault, kidnapping, or voluntary manslaughter, s/he will be charged as an adult if s/he used a deadly weapon during the commission of the offense or has previously been adjudicated delinquent for any of these offenses.[4]

According to the U.S. Census Bureau, approximately 24 percent of the population of Pennsylvania is under the age of 18.[5] The 2003 *Uniform Crime Reports* states that a total of 103,922 juveniles were arrested in Pennsylvania, making up approximately 25 percent of all persons arrested in the state. Approximately 18 percent of these juveniles (18,808) were arrested for Part I crimes. Seventy-five percent of the juvenile Part I crime arrests were for property crimes and 25 percent were for violent crimes.[6] Of the arrested juveniles, approximately 30 percent were handled by the police department and then released, 37 percent were referred to the juvenile justice system, 33 percent were referred to criminal or adult court, and the remainder (less than 1 percent) were referred to welfare agencies or to other police agencies.[7]

WHAT HAPPENS TO A JUVENILE WHO IS ARRESTED IN FLORIDA?

In Pennsylvania, juvenile justice services are operated at the county level, by county juvenile courts and juvenile probation offices. The juvenile justice system differs in several key ways from the adult criminal justice system. If a juvenile is taken into custody by the police (or any other person), the juvenile's parent or guardian must be notified "with all reasonable speed and without first taking the child elsewhere."[8] Juveniles 10 years of age or older who have been arrested for an act that if committed by an adult would be a felony or misdemeanor may be photographed and fingerprinted. However, if the juvenile is not adjudicated delinquent, the fingerprints and photographs must be immediately destroyed.[9]

After being taken into custody, a juvenile may be securely detained at a police station for no more than six hours. **Secure detention** involves being confined in a locked cell or other room, or being handcuffed to a stationary object such as a rail. However, the child may be kept in police custody for a longer period of time under less secure and confining conditions.[10] The primary reason for detaining the juvenile at the police station should be only for the

> purpose of identification, investigation, processing, releasing or transferring the child to a parent, guardian, other custodian, or juvenile court or county detention center and youth official, or to a shelter care or juvenile detention center.[11]

After the juvenile is processed, s/he will either be released into the custody of a parent or guardian or detained at a juvenile detention center until the detention hearing. However, unless at least one of the following conditions exist, the juvenile may not be detained prior to the detention hearing:

- detention is necessary to protect the child, the child's property, or the person or property of another

- there is reason to believe that the child will abscond (run away) or be taken out of the court's jurisdiction

- the juvenile has no parent, guardian, or custodian to provide care and supervision.[12]

If the juvenile is detained, a **petition** must be made to the court within 24 hours (or on the next business day of the court) after the child was admitted to the detention center or shelter care.[13] An informal **detention hearing** must be held within 72 hours to determine if there is probable cause to believe that the juvenile committed the delinquent act with which s/he is charged and whether or not the juvenile should be detained or placed under some other form of pretrial supervision.[14] If the juvenile is not detained, a **delinquency petition** must still be filed with the court to start the court process. In addition to the child's name, age, and address, and the names and addresses of the parents or guardians, the petition must state "that it is in the best interest of the child and the public that the proceeding be brought and, if delinquency is alleged, that the child is in need of treatment, supervision, or rehabilitation.[15]

Prior to filing the petition, an officer of the court (such as a probation officer) may determine that an **informal adjustment** would be more appropriate for the child. An informal adjustment, or **diversion**, usually lasts up to six months. If the conditions of the adjustment are fulfilled successfully by the child the charges against the child are withdrawn and there is no determination of guilt or innocence. However, if the juvenile violates the terms of the informal adjustment (e.g., by being arrested on new charges during the adjustment period), the state may file a delinquency petition on the original offense and initiate court proceedings against the juvenile.[16]

It is also possible to suspend the judicial process after the delinquency petition has been filed by entering a **consent degree**. Under a consent degree, the juvenile will be allowed to return to his or her home but will be kept under supervision under conditions determined by the probation officer. A consent decree usually lasts for six months, although the court has the option of extending it for an additional six months or of discharging the child early. This process is similar to an informal adjustment in that if the terms of the consent decree are completed successfully, there is no determination of guilt or innocence and the child will not have a formal juvenile record.[17]

If there is no informal adjustment or consent decree, the juvenile will be brought before the court for an **adjudicatory hearing**, which is the equivalent of a bench trial in adult court. If the child is being held in pretrial detention, the hearing must take place no more than ten days after the initial petition was filed. However, under certain conditions, the judge has the right to order the child to be detained for an additional period of up to ten days.[18]

The purpose of the adjudicatory hearing is to determine whether the juvenile committed the acts with which s/he has been charged. During the hearing, both the prosecution and the defense may present witness testimony and other evidence to the judge, who is responsible for determining whether or not the prosecution has proven the case beyond a reasonable doubt and, if so, whether the child needs treatment, supervision, or rehabilitation. If the judge decides the child is not in need of treatment, supervision, or rehabilitation, a finding of delinquency will be entered into the record and the proceedings will be dismissed. However, if the child was adjudicated delinquent for an act that, if committed by an adult, would be classified as a felony, the need for treatment, supervision, or rehabilitation is assumed. If the juvenile is found not delinquent, the court will dismiss the petition and the juvenile will immediately be released from any restrictions.[19]

If the juvenile is adjudicated delinquent by the court, and found to be in need of treatment, supervision, or rehabilitation, s/he may be held in detention while awaiting **disposition** of the case. During the **disposition hearing**, which is basically the equivalent of a sentencing hearing in adult court, the judge determines what type of disposition is appropriate for the juvenile and orders the appropriate placement or needed services. The hearing may be held on the same day as the adjudication hearing or at a later date, but it must take place no more than 20 days after the adjudication hearing.[20] Possible dispositions include:

- allowing the juvenile to remain at home with parents or guardians while meeting certain court-ordered conditions (e.g., participation in counseling, regular school attendance)

- assigning the juvenile to a period of supervised probation

- placing the juvenile in a community-based placement (a group home)

- committing the juvenile to an institution, camp, or other facility for delinquent children

- ordering the child to pay reasonable amounts of money (for fines, costs, or victim restitution)

- ordering the child to participate in some program of community service

The court may not place a juvenile in an adult institution unless the s/he has been convicted as an adult offender.[21]

The period of disposition may not be longer than is necessary to provide needed treatment or rehabilitation services. Institutional confinement may last no more than four years, or the period of time that an adult convicted of the same offense would receive, whichever is shorter. The court is required to review each commitment every six months and hold a **disposition review hearing** every nine months. At this review hearing, the judge has the option of changing the original disposition to better meet the treatment goals of the juvenile.[22]

It is important to remember that an adjudication of delinquency is not the same as a criminal conviction. Although there are some circumstances in which a delinquency adjudication may be used against an individual in a later judicial proceeding, a juvenile disposition order:

> does not impose any civil disability ordinarily resulting from a conviction or operate
> to disqualify the child in any civil service application or appointment.[23]

YOUTH COURT

Youth Court programs allow juvenile offenders to be sentenced by a jury of their peers, rather than in official juvenile court. Youth courts, which are also known as **teen courts** or **peer juries**, are not trial courts but they do help to reduce the pressure on the regular juvenile justice system. Youth courts are a form of **restorative justice**, which emphasizes the involvement of the offender, victim, and community in creating or restoring justice. Offenders are expected to work towards repairing the harm created by the crime and the harm done to victims. Other examples of restorative justice programs are victim/offender mediation, sentencing circles, and family group conferencing.

Pennsylvania currently has thirteen youth court programs.[24] The first was established in 1982 in Erie County and is operated by the county's Juvenile Probation Department. The purpose of the **Erie County Peer Jury Program** is to provide less serious juvenile offenders the opportunity to be diverted from the formal juvenile court into a peer adjudication program. Offenders are "tried" by a jury of their peers, rather than by the juvenile court. Participation in the program is voluntary but each participating juvenile offender must have the consent and attendance of a parent or guardian and must sign a formal admission of guilt for the charged offenses. Because of this, there is no issue of guilty or innocence. The peer jury, which is made up of 12 to 14 high school students, focuses on determining the appropriate disposition for the juvenile offender. Cases are heard in a courtroom setting and all dispositions available through the juvenile court, with the exceptions of probation and placement, are possible options for the teen jury. Common dispositions include requiring offenders to apologize to victims, write essays, observe curfews, and make restitution. The offender enters into a contract with the peer jury and is monitored by the juvenile probation department until s/he has completed the contract. Juveniles who are diverted into the peer jury program, and go through the program successfully, will have no official record of delinquency with the juvenile court. A juvenile who fails to complete the contract successfully may be remanded to the juvenile court for formal processing.[25]

NOTES

1. 42 Pa.C.S. §6302
2. *Ibid*
3. *Ibid*
4. *Ibid*
5. U.S. Census Bureau (http://www.census.gov)
6. *Uniform Crime Reports*, (http://www.fbi.gov/ucr/ucr.htm)
7. *Crime in Pennsylvania: Annual Uniform Crime Report, 2003*. Available online at: http://ucr.psp.state.pa.us/UCR/Reporting/Annual/AnnualFrames.asp?year=2003
8. 42 Pa.C.S. §6326(a)
9. 42 Pa.C.S.§6308(c)
10. 42 Pa.C.S. §6326(c)
11. *Ibid*
12. 42 Pa.C.S. §6325
13. 42 Pa.C.S. §6331
14. 42 Pa.C.S. §6332
15. 42 Pa.C.S. §6334(a)(1)
16. 42 Pa.C.S. §6323
17. 42 Pa.C.S. §6340

18.   42 Pa.C.S. §6335(a)
19.   42 Pa.C.S. §6341
20.   *Ibid*
21.   42 Pa.C.S. §6352
22.   42 Pa.C.S. §6353
23.   42 Pa.C.S. §6354(a)
24.   National Youth Court Center website (http://www.youthcourt.net/default.htm)
25.   Clouser, Megan (1996, November).   "Teen court/peer jury: A positive model of peer pressure." *Pennsylvania Progress*, v.3, #5, pp.1-5. Available online at: http://www.pccd.state.pa.us/pccd/LIB/pccd/pubs/progress/nov96.pdf

CHAPTER 10

DRUGS AND CRIME IN PENNSYLVANIA

INTRODUCTION

Drug abuse is a serious problem in Pennsylvania. The 2002 National Household Study on Drug Abuse found that 7.59 percent of persons 12 or older in Pennsylvania reported using an illicit drug in the past month. Recent drug use was most commonly reported among young adults between the ages of 18 and 25, with approximately 22 percent reporting past month illicit drug use. Approximately 12 percent of persons between the ages of 12 and 17, and 5 percent of persons 26 years or older reported the use of illicit drugs in the past month.[1]

In addition, 2.61 percent of those surveyed reported dependence or abuse of illicit drugs. Again, this was most common among younger persons, with approximately 6 percent of juveniles between 12 and 17, and 8 percent of those between 18 and 25 reporting abuse or dependence. Only approximately 1.3 percent of adults over the age of 25 reported dependence or abuse of illicit drugs.[2]

A recent study conducted in Philadelphia by the Drug Abuse Warning Network found that in 2002, about 1 percent of the approximately 1.9 million visits to hospital emergency rooms in the city were related to drug abuse. The drugs most commonly involved were cocaine, alcohol, marijuana, heroin, and benzodiazepines. Cocaine was a major problem; the rate of cocaine-related emergency room visits in Philadelphia in 2002 was 274 per 100,000, more than three times the national rate of 78. The rate of marijuana, heroin, and benzodizepine-related visits were also significantly higher than the national rate.[3]

During 2003, a total of 47,438 arrests for drug abuse violations were reported to the Federal Bureau of Investigation, including 40,968 adult arrests and 6,470 juvenile arrests. The number of drug arrests has decreased by 48,674 from the previous year.[4] According to the Pennsylvania Department of Correction (DOC), approximately 70 percent of all inmates admitted to the DOC are alcohol and/or drug dependent.[5]

In addition to arrests made by Pennsylvania law enforcement officers, the Drug Enforcement Agency (DEA) reported a total of 805 drug arrests in Pennsylvania during 2001. This is a decrease over the 2000 figure of 1,004 DEA drug arrests in the state.[6]

THE AVAILABILITY OF DRUGS IN PENNSYLVANIA

Marijuana

Marijuana is readily available throughout Pennsylvania. Most marijuana comes from Mexico or the southwestern border region of the United States.[7] Marijuana produced in from other states, Canada, and Jamaica is also available, as is locally produced marijuana. In FY 2003, the price of marijuana ranged from $80 to $225 per ounce and $5 to $35 a bag.[8] It is most commonly used by adults, although it is also popular among high school and college students. The drug is often smoked in combination with crack cocaine, heroin, or PCP.[9]

Cocaine

Cocaine, both powder and crack, appears to be the drug of choice for many users in Pennsylvania, particularly in Philadelphia and Pittsburgh. The primary source of cocaine in the state is New York City.[10] During FY 2003, **powder cocaine** sold for between $800 and $1,600 per ounce and between $28 and $125 per gram. Purity levels ranged from 60 to 95 percent. Powder cocaine is easily converted into **crack cocaine**, which sold for $3 to $50 a rock, at purity levels of approximately 80 percent.[11]

Heroin

Heroin is considered to be the most serious drug threat in Pennsylvania.[12] The primary source is New York City. Heroin is becoming increasingly popular among teens and young adults throughout the state and is used either alone or in combination with alcohol or cocaine (which frequently results in death from overdose).[13] During FY 2003, heroin purity levels ranged from 40 to 95 percent. Heroin prices during that period ranged from $2,000 to $6,500 per ounce and $10 to $50 a bag.[14]

Methamphetamine

Methamphetamine abuse is becoming an increasingly serious problem in Pennsylvania, although the availability of the drug is limited compared to other parts of the country. However, it appears that small methamphetamine laboratories are appearing in rural parts of the state, as well as in urban and suburban areas.[15] During FY 2003, methamphetamine in Pennsylvania sold for between $80 and $200 a gram, at purity levels ranging from 25 to 60 percent.[16]

Club Drugs

Club drugs include a variety of illegal drugs that are found at nightclubs and rave parties and on college and university campuses. The most common club drug in Pennsylvania is MDMA (Ecstacy), although GHB (gamma hydroxybutyric acid), its precursor GBL (gamma butyrlactone), and ketamine are also available, particularly in Philadelphia. The main source of MDMA in

Pennsylvania is New York City, although the drug is also smuggled into the state from the Netherlands by Israeli and Dutch Nationals and by members of Russian and Israeli organized crime groups.[17] During FY 2003, MDMA retailed for $9 to $35 a tablet while GHB sold for $10 to $20 per dosage unit.[18]

STATE SUBSTANCE ABUSE PROGRAMS

Office of Mental Health and Substance Abuse Services

The **Office of Mental Health and Substance Abuse Services** is located within the **Pennsylvania Department of Public Welfare**. The Office provides a variety of services to help individuals with substance abuse problems. These programs are offered to both children and adults in collaboration with the Pennsylvania Department of Health's Bureau of Drug and Alcohol Programs.[19]

Bureau of Drug and Alcohol Programs

The **Pennsylvania Department of Health's Bureau of Drug and Alcohol Programs** (BDAP) was created by the Pennsylvania Drug and Alcohol Abuse Control Act of 1972. It is responsible for:

> developing and implementing a comprehensive health, education, and rehabilitation
> program for the prevention, intervention, treatment and case management of drug and
> alcohol abuse and dependence.[20]

The BDAP had grant agreements with county level drug and alcohol commissions or programs, known as Single County Authorities (SCAs). There are 49 SCAs in Pennsylvania. Each SCA contracts with private service providers to provide a variety of drug and alcohol treatment and prevention services to county residents. The BDAP acts as a central oversight agency for the SCAs, who in turn provide administrative oversight for the contracted programs in the county.[21]

The Montgomery County Office of Drug and Alcohol Programs

The **Montgomery County Office of Drug and Alcohol Programs** is an example of an SCA. Through contracts with qualified local providers, the Office provides prevention services to approximately 6,000 county residents, through a variety of drug and alcohol awareness programs. These are available to all county residents. The Office also provides short-term counseling to approximately 3,500 county residents and ongoing in- and out-patient treatment to approximately 1,500 residents. Treatment preference is given to:

- pregnant IV drug users
- pregnant substance abusers
- injecting drug users[22]

PENNSYLVANIA DRUG COURTS

One new approach to breaking the cycle of drugs and crime is the concept of treatment-based drug courts. This approach, which was first developed in Florida in the late 1980s, quickly spread to other states, including Pennsylvania. As of May 2004, there were six drug courts in Pennsylvania that had been in operation for at least two years, five that had been implemented more recently, and seven in the planning stages.[23]

A drug court is a special court which handles cases involving drug-addicted offenders through the use of extensive supervision and treatment. The court also increases the coordination of various agencies and resources available to drug abusers, increasing the cost-effectiveness of the programs and providing the offender with access to a wide variety of programs and resources. Some drug courts are designed to handle adult offenders while others focus on juveniles.

Chester County Drug Court Program

The **Chester County Drug Court Program** is designed to divert non-violent drug dependant offenders from trial by providing alternatives to traditional criminal justice prosecution for drug-related offenses. To participate in the program, an offender must be charged with a non-mandatory drug offense and/or a first offense DUI with a drug offense. Offenders who are under parole or probation supervision or who have a prior record for a violent offense are not eligible for the program. All participants must be legal residents of the U.S., must waive their right to a preliminary hearing, and must be undergo a drug and alcohol assessment prior to being considered for the program.[24] If the offender is accepted into the program, the court will impose a pretrial disposition, known as a "Disposition in Lieu of Trial or Criminal Punishment."[25]

The program lasts from one to two years and involves four phases of supervision. Each offender is assigned to a probation officer and is expected to comply with all program rules and regulations, undergo regular drug and alcohol testing, attend all mandated treatment programs, appear before the drug court for review, pay all fines and costs, and be involved in a productive daily activity (e.g., work or school). During the first phase of the program, offenders must under go drug screenings twice per week and appear before the court weekly. As an offender successfully completes assigned conditions and stays drug- or alcohol-free, s/he is moved to later phases and the program requirements are reduced.

After an offender successfully completes all four phases of the drug court program, stays sober for 90 consecutive days, successfully completes all treatment goals, completes a phase three project, and pays all fines and costs, s/he may be eligible for graduation from the program. When the offender successfully completes the drug court program, the charges are dismissed and the record of the crime are expunged. However, If an offender consistently and repeatedly violates program requirements, s/he may be removed from the drug court program and prosecuted in criminal court on the original charges.[26]

NOTES

1. Substance Abuse and Mental Health Services Administration (SAMHSA) - State data on alcohol, tobacco, and illicit drug use. Available online at: http://oas.samhsa.gov/states.htm

2. *Ibid*

3. Drug Abuse Warning Network (2004, January). *The DAWN Report. Highlights from DAWN: Philadelphia 2002.* Available online at: http://dawninfo.samhsa.gov/pubs_94_02/shortreports/metro/files/Philly_TDR.pdf

4. *Uniform Crime Reports*, (http://www.fbi.gov/ucr/ucr.htm)

5. Pennsylvania Department of Corrections (2003, March 14). *Drug Treatment Alternative-To-Prison (DTAP) Program.* Available online at: http://www.cor.state.pa.us/stats/lib/stats/DTAP.pdf

6. Office of National Drug Control Policy (2004, May). *State of Pennsylvania: Profile of Drug Indicators.* (http://www.whitehousedrugpolicy.gov/statelocal/pa/pa.pdf)

7. DEA Fact Sheet: *Pennsylvania* (http://www.usdoj.gov/dea/pubs/states/pennsylvania.html)

8. Office of National Drug Control Policy (2004, May). *State of Pennsylvania: Profile of Drug Indicators, op cit.*

9. DEA Fact Sheet: *Pennsylvania, op cit.*

10. *Ibid*

11. Office of National Drug Control Policy (2004, May). *State of Pennsylvania: Profile of Drug Indicators, op cit.*

12. *Ibid*

13. DEA Fact Sheet: *Pennsylvania, op cit.*

14. Office of National Drug Control Policy (2004, May). *State of Pennsylvania: Profile of Drug Indicators, op cit.*

15. DEA Fact Sheet: *Pennsylvania, op cit.*

16. Office of National Drug Control Policy (2004, May). *State of Pennsylvania: Profile of Drug Indicators, op cit.*

17. DEA Fact Sheet: *Pennsylvania, op cit.*

18. Office of National Drug Control Policy (2004, May). *State of Pennsylvania: Profile of Drug Indicators, op cit.*

19. Pennsylvania Department of Public Welfare web site (http://www.dpw.state.pa.us/)

20. Pennsylvania Department of Health web site (http://www.dsf.health.state.pa.us/health/site/default.asp)

21. *Ibid*

22. Mongtomery County Office of Drug and Alcohol Programs web site (http://www.montcopa.org/mhmrda/webformhmrda/DA/DAHome.htm)

23. Office of Justice Programs, Drug Court Clearinghouse and Technical Assistance Project (200, May 27). *Summary of Drug Court Activity by State and County.* Available online at: http://spa.american.edu/justice/publications/drgchart2k.pdf

24. Chester County Adult Probation and Parole web site (http://www.chesco.org/adprob/)

25. 35 P.S. §780-118

26. Chester County Adult Probation and Parole web site, *op cit.*

APPENDIX

WEB SITES OF INTEREST

There is a wealth of information on Pennsylvania and the Pennsylvania criminal justice system available on the World Wide Web. Below are a selection of web sites that may be of interest to students.

GENERAL PENNSYLVANIA WEB SITES AND LEGAL INFORMATION

http://www.state.pa.us/
> The official web site of the Commonwealth of Pennsylvania. This site provides a variety of information services for citizens and for state and local government.

http://www.dgs.state.pa.us/pamanual/site/default.asp
> The web site for Volume 116 of the *Pennsylvania Manual*.

http://members.aol.com/StatutesPA/Index.html
> A web site which contains some (but not all) of the Pennsylvania Consolidated and Unconsolidated Statues. It also contains links to the Pennsylvania Rules of Court, Pennsylvania Rules of Evidence, and other useful links.

http://www.legis.state.pa.us/
> The official home page of the Pennsylvania General Assembly.

http://sites.state.pa.us/govlocal.html?papowerPNavCtr=|30207|#30214
> This web page provides links to many county and local government web sites in Pennsylvania.

INFORMATION ON POLICE IN PENNSYLVANIA

http://www.psp.state.pa.us/
> The web site of the Pennsylvania State Police.

http://www.ppdonline.org/ppd_home.htm
> The web site of the City of Philadelphia Police Department.

http://derrycops.com/index.html
> The web site of the Derry Township Police Department.

http://www.eriecountysheriffs.org/
>   The web site for the Erie County Sheriff's Office.

http://www.publicsafety.upenn.edu/default.asp
>   The web site of the University of Pennsylvania Division of Public Safety.

http://www.mpoetc.state.pa.us/mpotrs/site/default.asp
>   The web site of the Municipal Police Officers' Education and Training Committee.

INFORMATION ON THE COURTS IN PENNSYLVANIA

http://www.courts.state.pa.us/
>   The web site of the Pennsylvania Unified Judicial System. This site includes information on all courts in the state.

http://www.pabarexam.org/Default.htm
>   The web site for the Pennsylvania Board of Law Examiners.

http://www.pabar.org/
>   The web site for the Pennsylvania Bar Association.

http://pcs.la.psu.edu/
>   The web site for the Pennsylvania Commission on Sentencing.

http://www.pccd.state.pa.us/pccd/site/default.asp
>   The web site for the Pennsylvania Commission on Crime and Delinquency.

INFORMATION ON CORRECTIONS IN PENNSYLVANIA

http://www.cor.state.pa.us/
>   The web site for the Pennsylvania Department of Corrections.

http://www.parole.state.pa.us/pbpp/site/default.asp
>   The web site of the Pennsylvania Board of Probation and Parole.

http://www.pci.state.pa.us/pci/site/
>   The web site for Pennsylvania Correctional Industries.

http://www.prisonsociety.org/index.html
>   The web site of the Pennsylvania Prison Society.

INFORMATION ON JUVENILE JUSTICE IN PENNSYLVANIA

http://www.jlc.org/default.htm
      The web site of the Juvenile Law Center.

http://www.dpw.state.pa.us/Child/ChildCare/003670346.htm
      The Office of Children, Youth, and Families.

INFORMATION ON DRUGS IN PENNSYLVANIA

http://www.whitehousedrugpolicy.gov/statelocal/pa/pa.pdf
      The Office of National Drug Control Policy provides a large amount of information on drug use statistics and drug prevention efforts in Pennsylvania.

http://www.usdoj.gov/dea/pubs/states/Pennsylvania.html
      A DEA fact sheet on drugs in Pennsylvania.